THE ROYAL HOTEL

by

Dell Winslade

To

Pam

A fellow lover of history!

Dell

First Published in Great Britain 2021
by World of Creative Dreams ®

54 St James Street
Liverpool
L1 0AB

worldofcreativedreams.co.uk

British Library Cataloguing in Publication Data.
A catalogue record for this book is available from the British Library.

ISBN 978 0 9935524 3 4

MUM

This book is dedicated to the lady who started to write this story. My Mother, Mabel Doreen Ford. She preferred to be called Doreen, but to my sister Amanda and me, she was Mum.

Mum was born in Liverpool and even though she had lived in Southampton for many years, she had never forgotten her Liverpool roots.

We made regular visits back to Liverpool with Mum over the years. Trips were made to the city's main library to get the family research, which would eventually inspire Mum to write her book.

Sadly, she never got the chance to complete this, so Amanda and I were able to finish this story for her. We hope we have done her proud.

This is for you, Mum.

With all our love,
Dell and Amanda.

x x

ROYAL HOTEL.
CHEMISTS
DAY & NIGHT
SERVICE

ROYAL HOTEL

The Royal stood in the middle of Lime Street, right in the centre of the city of Liverpool. It was a busy hotel with five bedrooms for guests and a public bar as well as the family rooms.

On the ground floor, there was a large public bar, a small lounge bar and a coffee lounge. The coffee lounge was used by ladies who would not go into the bar. In there, they could take a drink or just have coffee. It was also used in the mornings by the guests for their breakfast. The floor of the coffee lounge sloped so badly, that the grandfather clock that stood in the corner never worked.

At the back of the ground floor, was a large kitchen and scullery. In the kitchen, Mother made her hot pots, a famous Lancashire dish made of meat, potatoes and onions.

On the first floor were the family rooms. In the front of the hotel was a large parlour with large windows overlooking Lime Street. At the back were the bedrooms. Father and Mother's room was large with a four-poster bed, a sofa and a fireplace. They would have a fire there in the winter. Mother liked to use this room to be quiet and to get away from the noise and bustle of the public rooms. She would sit by the fire and knit or sew. It was her time to be by herself and the children respected this.

Daughter Mabel had a small bedroom to herself and the three boys shared a large room.

On the second floor were the five guest bedrooms; two large rooms at the front and three small ones at the back.

Over the years of this story, the city of Liverpool would be affected by events both before and during World War One. For the family who lived in and work at the Royal Hotel, they too would get involved as well as having their own stories to tell.

This is their story.

THE FAMILY

The Royal Hotel is the home of the Winslade family. Father is Henry but he is known to everyone as Harry. He is a tall man with a kind face. He is firm but fair and well respected.

Mother is Jane. She is a loving person, only seeing the best in people. She is tall and has dark hair which she wears in a coil on top of her head. Mother is well known for her cooking, especially her hot pots.

There are four Winslade children. The eldest is Mabel and in this year 1911, she is 10 years old. She has long red hair which she wears with a ribbon bow at the back of her neck. Mabel has a temper and is bossy towards her brothers. In fact, she has a scar on her left thumb from when her brother Bill, who had had enough one day, stuck a fork into her hand.

Tommy is the eldest boy. He is 8 years old. He is a quiet lad and close to Mabel. With his fair hair and pale face, he looks sensitive and not very strong.

Bill is 7 years old. He is noisy, adventurous and always in trouble. He has a fascination for ships and the sea and says that one day, he will sail around the world. He also sings in the cathedral choir and looks angelic, which is a bit unsettling as you wonder what he is going to do next.

Fred is the youngest and at 5 years old, he is a tubby and happy child. He will follow his brothers everywhere as Fred always wants to know about everything. He is always asking questions such as *'what is that and what does it do?'* or *'what is this?'* Fred also has a passion for cats. The three Royal cats are called George, Jasper and Smokie. They follow him about and are always waiting for him when he comes home from school.

As well as the family, there are hotel staff. The only one who lives at the hotel is Robert who is a barman, night porter and a handyman. Robert has a small room at the back of the bar.

Kate is the housemaid and Alice the kitchen maid, and then there is Mrs Hanley who is the cleaner. Now, Mrs Hanley has a drink problem. She will go about her work with a bottle of gin hidden in her basket, in with the polish and dusters.

Mother knew about this, but she felt sorry for the old lady and ignored it, even though it left Mother having to do some of the work again.

Over the next few years, the family will all see a part of history happening in the city of Liverpool. There will be laughter and tears, happiness and sorrow.

All a part of life.

L-R: Tommy, Mabel and Jane.

Portrait of Jane.

ST. LUKE'S SCHOOL

Mabel tried to hurry the boys along. She was going to be late for her class again. She would always try to slip in without her teacher seeing her, but Mr Parry would catch her and say to her in a loud voice.

"Late again! Mabel."

Mabel hated it but she had to look after her brothers and make sure they were safe in school. Tommy was a great help to her. He was the sensible one.

Mabel took hold of Fred's hand to cross the busy road. She was also carrying her large bag with her school books and her lunch box in. The boys carried their books in a strap across their shoulders and Tommy carried their lunches. The children hurried along Lime Street towards St. Luke's.

It wasn't a very large school but the children were very mixed with children both from the wealthy families and the poor. It was a dark building made of grey stone and with small windows. There was a small playground with benches for the children to sit and have their lunches in the summer. In winter, they stayed in their classrooms.

The classrooms were small and held about 20 children who sat at small wooden desks on hard wooden chairs. The desks had large lids and inside were paper and pencils for the children.

As well as their normal classes, the girls went to a laundry centre one day a week where they were taught cookery, laundry, childcare and housewifery. This was because some of the girls would go into domestic service. The fact that Mabel lived in a hotel, of course, meant that these classes were very useful. Although, she did learn most of these things by watching Mother.

Mabel's best friend at school was Daisy. Daisy came from a poor family and although she was the same age as Mabel, she was small, thin and undernourished. Mabel had told Mother about Daisy so when Mother made Mabel's lunch, she would put extra sandwiches in for Daisy.

Mabel saw the boys to their class and then hurried to her own. She was on time this morning. She sighed with relief. Before going in, she put her red hair into place and smoothed her skirt and long-sleeved floral blouse. She opened the door and hurried to her seat.

Mr Parry looked over his glasses at her and smiled. Then, he tapped his desk with a large ruler for quiet to start class. Mabel had a look for Daisy who always sat at the back of the classroom out of the way of the other children. She was there. Mabel gave her a quick wave and Daisy smiled back.

The bell rang when it was lunchtime. The children all shut their desk lids with a bang and rushed to the door.

"Quiet please!" yelled Mr Parry, but everyone rushed out.

Daisy waited for Mabel and the two girls walked out into the playground to find a seat. Mabel carried her lunch box with the sandwiches. Mabel shared out the sandwiches. Daisy ate hers, looking around. She was very quiet and looked worried.

"Daisy, what is wrong?" asked Mabel.

Daisy put her sandwich on her lap and burst into tears.

"It's Butch Jenkins," she sobbed. "He keeps bullying me. It is because of the way I look," she whispered.

Daisy looked down at her shoes. The holes were covered with paper. Her dress was a size too big where it had come from a charity and it wasn't very clean.

Boris 'Butch' Jenkins was the school bully. He was a plump, ugly-looking boy. Most of the small children were terrified of him as he used his looks and size to frighten them.

Mabel took a clean hanky from her pocket.

"Spit on it," she told Daisy. Daisy did as she was told and Mabel wiped her friend's face, which by this time was really dirty with the tears running down her cheeks.

Mabel was determined to find out what was really wrong with her friend.

"Is there something else making you unhappy?" she asked.

Daisy dried her eyes and nodded.

"I have to leave here and go to a special school," she said.

"What do you mean, a special school?" Mabel asked, puzzled.

"For poor people," said Daisy. She was quietly looking around, making sure that no one would hear her. Mabel was just about to ask what she meant when there was a grunt.

"Well! Look here. It's little poor girl and her friend," yelled Butch Jenkins.

The two girls looked up in horror. Butch was standing in front of them with a nasty look on his podgy face.

Daisy grabbed Mabel's arm but even though she was scared and her legs were shaking, Mabel stood up and clinched her fist.

"Leave us alone you bully!" she shouted at Butch, who laughed at her.

"If I don't, what are you going to do about it?" he snarled.

At that moment, Butch jumped and spun round. Bill was kicking him in the legs. Fred, seeing what his brother was doing, joined in kicking Butch in the ankles. Butch was just going to hit out at the two boys when he saw Tommy standing in front of him. He stood tall and faced the bully.

"Leave those girls alone, Jenkins," he said in a quiet but firm voice. "Pick on someone your own size. You are a bully and a coward." Tommy was shaking but he stood firm.

Butch gave a nasty laugh and shaking the two small boys away from him, he swaggered towards his friends who were watching everything with interest.

At that moment, the teacher rang the bell to tell the children, dinnertime was over.

Mabel took Daisy's hand and they walked towards the door followed by the boys. As they passed Butch, he hissed at them.

"You Winslades," he snarled. "You think you're someone don't you? But I will get you. You see if I don't." With that, he pushed past them to the door.

After school, Daisy looked for her two younger brothers. She found them being tormented as usual because of their ragged clothes. She took their hands and they all ran along the road. When they got to the corner, she turned and waved at Mabel.

When Mabel and the boys got home, she went to find Mother who was in the kitchen, preparing the evening meal.

"Mother, do you know anything about a school for poor children?" she asked. "Daisy said she has to go there and she is very unhappy about it."

Mother wiped her hands on the towel and thought for a moment.

"Yes dear," she started to explain. "I have heard about them but not much I'm afraid. They are called industrial schools for children from deprived homes."

"What does deprived mean?" asked Mabel, puzzled. "And what is the difference between them and us?"

Mother sat down at the table.

"Sit down dear and I will try to explain," she said.

Mother thought about how she would tell her daughter about her friend. She knew that Mabel would miss Daisy very much.

"Daisy comes from a very poor family," said Mother. "You know that, don't you?"

Mabel nodded. Mother sighed and, taking Mabel's hand, she went on.

"Daisy's father does not have a job," Mother explained. "He does not work and so there is not much money for them and they do not have all the things that you have here. Nice clothes, good home and plenty to eat, so they are a deprived family."

"But why send her to another school. What difference does that make?" asked Mabel. She was really upset. She only saw Daisy at school because Mother would not let her go to Daisy's home.

One thing Mother did know about Daisy's new school was that the parents of these children would not always send them to school and so by sending them to this special school, the Education Board could keep an eye on their attendance.

Mother looked at her daughter's unhappy face and had a thought. She smiled.

"Why don't we have Daisy and her brothers to tea here one day soon?" she suggested. "We can have sandwiches and you can help me make cakes. We can have ice cream and sweets."

Mabel's face changed to a happy one and she clapped her hands.

"Oh! That sounds wonderful," she laughed with excitement.

Mabel jumped up from the table and going to her Mother, she gave her a hug. Then, she rushed from the kitchen to find the boys. Mother sighed and went back to her meal. She thought about children like Daisy and wondered what the future would hold for them.

THE RIOT

SUNDAY 13TH AUGUST 1911

Mabel skipped down the stairs to the kitchen. It was Sunday morning and the sun was shining. It was going to be a lovely day. She was wearing one of her new dresses. It was a green and white floral dress which went down to her ankles and she wore her new white button boots. She wondered what they could do today.

Just as she was about to push open the kitchen door, it suddenly swung back and Alice, the kitchen maid, came through with breakfast on a tray for two of the guests. She scowled at Mabel, but then, Alice scowled at everyone in her dark grey dress and white apron and her hair falling out of her white cap. Alice always looked angry. Mabel ignored her and went into the kitchen. Mother was pouring hot water from a huge kettle into two brown teapots. A tall lady, Mother looked serious with her hair pulled back into a bun, but when she smiled, her face lit up.

"Hello dear," she said, happy to see her daughter. "How are you today?"

She went on putting the teapots on a tray with cups, saucers, milk and sugar. Before Mabel could answer, the door opened again with force. It was Bill.

"Guess what!" he shouted. "There is a policeman in the hall talking to Father. I'm going to listen. Something is going on."

With that, he rushed out again, nearly knocking Alice over who was coming back for the tea.

Bill hid in the dark corner of the hall so he could hear the conversation between his Father and the Police Sergeant.

"So you see, Mr Winslade," said the Sergeant. "It would be better if you still opened up the bar as usual but you should have some help."

"You know what I mean," he said. He smiled and went on. "A couple of hefty men in case of any trouble."

"Yes!" Father nodded to agree. "I have already thought of that. Robert, my barman, has two brothers. Quite strapping lads by all account, who can handle themselves if fighting starts."

"Good," the Sergeant sighed. "I wish this was not happening but it is. I am afraid my men will need help. We are thinking of extra men. Also, the army will be involved."

The Sergeant sighed again.

"I will be glad when this day is all over," he said.

Bill edged his way back towards the kitchen. As soon as he was out of sight of the two men, he rushed back through the kitchen door.

"There is going to be a war in Lime Street!" he shouted. "The Army are coming."

Mabel looked at her Mother.

"Oh, Mother!" she gasped. "Is that true?"

Mother took Bill by the arm and pushed him to the table.

"Now sit down young man and be quiet," she said, annoyed with her son. "You are frightening your sister."

"You are going to have to stay home today," Mother explained to Mabel and Bill. "It will not be safe for you to be outside."

"But the Army," asked Mabel. "What are they doing here?"

Mother sighed. Pouring herself a cup of tea, she sat at the table with the children.

"I will try and explain so you understand," she said.

Taking a drink of her tea, she asked them, "Do you know what a strike is?"

"You hit people," said Bill, waving his arm in the air to demonstrate.

"No dear," Mother continued. "A strike is when people refuse to work because of all sorts of reasons. This one is because of poor wages and very bad houses that these people have to live in. It started with the seamen's demands for a union. It has spread to the men who work on the railway, on the docks and in the warehouses. Now, a union is a group of people who will look after the workmen and help them when they need it, such as trying to get them better wages so they can find better places for their families to live."

Mabel nodded and she thought about Daisy who lived in a tenement building in a poor part of the city. Her father had worked in the docks. Mabel could understand the need for better houses for the families.

As Mother paused to drink her tea, Mabel looked around the large kitchen. The windows looked out at the back of the hotel onto the alley between the hotel and Lime Street railway station. The room was bright and cheerful. The family had their meals at the large wooden table, except for special days such as Christmas when they used the dining table in the parlour. The kitchen was painted in green and cream. In the corner was a large Welsh dresser. It was made of dark wood. On hooks hung copper pans and there were heavy china dishes on the shelves.

Mother was well known in the city for her hot pots which she cooked in the new electric cooker Father had put in. It was so new that not many people had one. Alice and Kate would not touch it for fear it would blow up but Mother also still liked to cook on her range oven which was warmed by the fire.

Suddenly, there was a knock on the back door making everyone jump.

Mabel opened the door and sighed with relief when she saw Robert's two brothers there.

"Morning Missus," the taller of the two men said. "I'm John and this is Tony."

He nodded towards his brother. Tony didn't say a word. He just grinned, showing that he didn't have many teeth. Mother shuddered and wondered if they had been knocked out in a fight.

The men took off their caps and walked into the kitchen. They were roughly dressed in heavy shirts, waistcoats and dark trousers that were tucked into heavy boots. They were dressed, ready for trouble.

Leaving their mother to make them a cup of tea, Mabel and Bill left the kitchen and made their way to the stairs. Bill rushed off to find Tommy and Fred. Mabel went into the parlour. The parlour windows overlooked Lime Street and St. George's Plateau. Mabel looked through the window. She could see that the crowds were gathering and already they were very large. She was just about to turn away when she heard crying outside. Opening the window a little but keeping back out of sight, she peeped out.

There was a young woman with two children by her side and a baby in her arms. One of the children, a boy about Bill's age was shouting at his Mother.

"I want to go with my Dad over there," he said, pointing at the Plateau.

"Oh! Do be quiet Johnny," the Mother said. "You can't. You will be hurt." She was trying to shush the little girl who was crying.

"I'm hungry!" the child cried.

"I know, sweetheart," her mother replied. "I will try and find some food for us. Come now, dry your eyes and be a big girl for Mum."

The mother pulled the shawl she had around her shoulders and wrapped it around the baby, hugging it close. She was dressed in a cotton shirt, shabby jacket and skirt. Her hair was pulled back from her face and looked unwashed. The children also looked shabby, their clothes not very clean and Mabel was horrified to see they were not wearing any shoes. The mother walked away with the two children behind her, the boy stamping his bare feet because he could not go to his father.

Mabel thought about all the food Mother had to throw away because they had too much. How could that be when there were people in the city hungry? Most of the poorer children were thin and undernourished. Many died before they reached their teens because of illness caused by dirty conditions and lack of food. There were ten or more children to a family and the older children would stand outside the back doors of hotels and wait for the food thrown away from the kitchens. They would gather what they could and take it home for their brothers and sisters. As well as being hungry, the children were infested with head lice. They played in dirty streets that were littered with rubbish and fouled by dirty and diseased dogs.

Mabel turned away from the window and she looked around at the parlour. It was a big room. There was a large sofa and two armchairs. There were rugs on the polished floor and pictures on the walls. On one side, there was a large dining table and chairs and also a sideboard on which stood the family photographs which Mother had had taken by the city photographer.

Mabel's thoughts were suddenly interrupted by a lot of

shouting outside. It was coming from the Plateau. She went back to the window and looked out. Hearing the noise, she could see that fighting had started. At that moment, the door opened and Bill rushed in followed by Tommy and Fred.

"I told them we are going to have a war outside!" Bill shouted.

"Can we watch?" Fred asked, excitably.

Mabel groaned and looked at Tommy.

"Never mind them," said Tommy. He was so thoughtful for his age. He put his arm around his sister.

"So what is happening?" he asked, going to the window.

Mabel told Tommy what Mother had said.

"I think Father is worried in case we have trouble here," she went on. "He has Robert's brothers here if he should need them and we have to stay upstairs don't we?"

She glared at Bill. Bill pulled a face and went on looking through the window.

As the children watched, the Mounted Police arrived to control the crowds but the fights were starting all over. Many people were going to be hurt. An ambulance pulled by two horses came around the corner from Market Street into Lime Street. A man was hanging on at the back, ringing the warning bell. Mabel watched in horror as he suddenly slipped and fell into the road. The crowd scattered to make way for the ambulance. The whole scene was looking very dangerous.

The door opened and Mother came in.

"It is getting very nasty out there," she said, going to the window.

Suddenly, there were screams and yelling. As Mother and the children watched, the Mounted Police charged the crowd to disperse the people. Fred, who was watching from another window, cried out and ran to Mother. She cradled him in her arms and then looked around.

"Where is Bill?" she asked.

"He went out," Fred stopped crying to say.

"Not outside," Mother said, horrified, "Oh! That boy!" She caught her breath. How had she not seen him leave the room?

"Tommy," Mother told him. "Run and tell Father that Bill may have gone outside. I will look in the bedrooms in case he is there."

Mother hurried along the landing towards the stairs. Just as she got there, Tommy who had rushed downstairs, shouted. At that moment, Father came from the bar to see what was going on. They all watched as Bill was going through the front door, closing it behind him.

Outside, standing on the step, Bill was just going to move when, suddenly, a mounted policeman on a large black horse was in front of him. The horse was startled by the screaming crowd and was prancing about as the policeman was trying to control it.

Bill was too frightened to move. His legs felt like they were made of wood.

Suddenly, the horse reared up on its hind legs. Bill screamed in terror. The front hooves seemed to be right on top of him.

Then, a strong pair of hands grabbed him by the shoulders and pulled him back through the door to safety. Father was red with anger and he shook the terrified boy.

"You little fool!" Father shouted. "You could have been killed or crippled for life. Now go to your bedroom and stay there for the rest of the day."

Bill ran up the stairs sobbing.

Mother came down to Father who was still shaking. He looked at her.

"That was very close, Jane," he said. "When will that child learn to do as he is told?"

Mother made her way back to the other children. Tommy

by this time had told Mabel and Fred what had happened. Fred was still crying and ran to Mother who sat down on the sofa and pulled him on to her lap.

"Now," sighed Mother, "Bill has been very silly today. He is staying in the bedroom where I hope he will think about what he did and what could have happened to him."

Later that evening, Father heard that there had been at least 30,000 people there during the riot. Everyone at the Royal had then gone to bed and Lime Street was quiet once more. Troops from the Royal Warwickshire Regiment had been involved in crowd control and were now on duty at the Plateau.

Father and Mother had retired to their bedroom. Father looked through the window at Lime Street and St. George's Plateau, which were covered with rubbish. He sighed and, turning away from the window, he looked around the bedroom. Families with children were living in just one room as big as this. He looked down at his dressing gown. The value of it would keep one of those families in food for a month. There was nothing he could do about it. This was the way things were. Father sighed again and looked at Mother.

"I wonder how long this dispute will last," he sighed. "I have a feeling it will be for a while and it will affect everyone."

"I was thinking about Bill," said Mother. "If that horse had come down on him, it could have broken his back." She started to cry. Father sat beside her and took her hand.

"But he wasn't hurt and I do not think we will ever cure his adventurous spirit," Father assured her. "He will go far and see places we never will. That, I am sure of, but for now, we will have to just keep an eye on him." He smiled and patted Mother's hand.

"We are lucky with our children, aren't we Harry?" asked Mother. "When I saw those poor souls out there today."

"Yes, we are lucky," he replied.

A little while later as they settled into their large comfortable bed, Mother thought about all the mothers who were going to sleep in the poor areas of the city. Living in dark and damp basements, their children dirty and hungry. She hoped that today was not in vain and that conditions would improve for these poor people.

In the early hours of the morning, the street cleaners with their brushes and wheelbarrows would start to clean up.

FRED

It was a warm morning. The children were all sitting down to breakfast. Fred, who was the last one to walk in, noticed that there were three dishes of cat food all side by side on the kitchen floor. Normally, when they knew they were being fed, all three cats would come running in. But, this time it was different. The cats all had collars with their names and the hotel on. So, if one of them were to go missing, hopefully people would bring them back.

When two of Fred's cats, Jasper and Smokie, came in and started eating, Fred noticed that the third one, George, hadn't followed them in.

Mother had just sat down to have breakfast with them when Fred suddenly jumped up out of his chair.

"What's the matter Fred?" asked Mother.

Mabel, Tommy and Bill stopped eating and looked at him. It seemed that no one had noticed that there were only two cats instead of three.

"Where's George?" Fred asked in a panic. "Has anybody seen him?"

"Maybe he's still outside enjoying the sunshine," said Mabel.

"But he always comes in and eats with the other two," said Fred. "Always."

"Don't worry, Fred," said Tommy. "He'll be back when he's ready."

“And what if he doesn’t come back?” Fred asked, getting rather anxious.

“Please dear, eat your breakfast,” said Mother.

Fred sat back down to try and eat his breakfast.

A few minutes passed. There was still one dish with cat food in it and still no sign of George. Fred was only halfway through his breakfast but he still couldn’t eat it. When he saw the two other cats lick up their dishes to finish and start to walk away, Fred decided that he could no longer just sit there. Again, he got up from his chair.

“You haven’t finished eating,” said Mother.

“I know and I’m sorry,” said Fred. “But I’m worried about him. I have to go out and try to find him.”

Understanding how worried he was, Mother knew he wouldn’t settle until he had found him.

“All right dear, you may go,” she said. “Please be careful out there crossing the road. It’s a busy road at this time of the morning.”

Fred wasted no more time. He dashed through the main corridor grabbing his coat on the way out.

“We want to help if that’s all right?” Mabel said to Mother.

“Of course you can,” said Mother. “Just make sure he crosses that road safely.”

As they walked out of the hotel, they could see Fred, who by now, was some way ahead heading up towards Seymour Street.

Fred crossed the busy road to get to that side of the street, being careful and looking both ways for traffic. Despite being careful while crossing, there was no doubt he was still worried about his missing cat.

The other three children all decided to follow him. They would occasionally stop people in the street and ask them if they had seen this cat, giving them a brief description. However, it seemed that nobody had seen him.

Suddenly, Tommy noticed from the other side of the road that Fred was waving his arms about.

"Look!" Tommy shouted to Mabel and Bill.

"I think he's found him," he said, pointing to Fred.

In this street were rows of houses on both sides. These were the type of houses that were lived in by well-off people. To the front of each house were fences and gates made of iron. Each fence had iron railings.

In the first house Fred came to, there was George. Somehow, he had managed to get across the road to here without getting hurt or worse. He was sitting in the front garden of this house, looking around almost as if he thought he lived there.

Fred was just glad to see him, no matter where he was. He peered through the iron railings. He tried to coax George to come closer.

After a few seconds, it seemed to be working. George stood up, purring away and started to move forward. Fred put his right arm through a gap in the railings, hoping to grab him. There was a railing missing so, the gap seemed to be bigger. He was so determined to get hold of him that, gradually, his head felt like it was coming through.

Suddenly, there was this noise from behind, like a loud bang. George was startled by the noise and backed away, just as Fred had his hand on him. Then, before Fred had time to stop himself, his whole head went through the gap.

Fred tried to get his head back through and then realised that he couldn't. He managed to wriggle his arm back through. With both hands, he grabbed hold of the railings on either side of him trying to force his head through, but it was in vain. His head was stuck.

Mabel, Tommy and Bill had just got across the road. When they reached the house, Mabel was horrified. She couldn't believe what she was seeing. Her youngest brother, kneeling down on the pavement with his head stuck in railings. Fred could just turn his head to see them there.

"Help me!" he shouted. "I'm stuck."

Bill ran towards Fred and grabbed him by the ankles. Tommy let himself through the gate with Mabel following him. She went up the steps and banged on the front door hoping that maybe, whoever lived there was home. There was no answer. She tried again.

"Hello!" she called through the letterbox. "Is there anyone home?"

Meanwhile, Tommy knelt down by Fred's face.

"I'm stuck," Fred repeated. "I can't get my head out."

He was starting to panic.

"You need to calm down Fred," Tommy said, trying to reassure him. Tommy put his hands on Fred's head.

"What are you doing?" Fred asked.

"Please just try and keep still," replied Tommy.

Mabel had no luck knocking on the door. It seemed that there was nobody home. She came back down the steps to join her brothers.

"I don't think there's anyone in," she said. "They must be out shopping."

"Please hurry up and do something!" Fred shouted.

"I've got his ankles," Bill shouted. "I'll pull and you push."

"Okay!" Tommy started to count. "On two. One! Two!"

Tommy pushed and Bill pulled. No matter how hard they tried, it didn't seem to be working. Fred started to cry out.

"Oh! Please stop," said Mabel. "You're hurting him."

"We must do something," said Bill.

Just as they were trying to think what to do next, a well-dressed, middle-aged couple came walking up the street towards them. Their hands were full of shopping.

Mabel came back out through the gate and approached them.

"Can you please help us?" she asked. "That's my brother. He has his head stuck."

"So I can see," the man replied in a quiet but calm voice.

"I don't know who lives here," Mabel said. "I tried knocking on the door but nobody answered."

"You're lucky," the man said. "It's us. We live here. This is my wife by the way."

"Hello!" she said.

"Well, then," the man smiled. "We can't leave your brother stuck here all day. Let's see what we can do."

He put his shopping down by his wife. Then, he went over to the lads to look at the situation.

"Tell me young man," he said, bending down to talk to Fred. "Are you hurt at all?"

"No! Sir," Fred huffed. "I'm not hurt. Just stuck. Please help."

As he looked up, he noticed one of the local policemen walking on the other side of the road. He could see the commotion so he crossed over. To the children's surprise, he knew the couple.

"Hello Peter," the Policeman said. "I see you have a young lad here in a spot of bother."

Mabel had decided that enough time had been wasted. She quickly told the lady what she was going to do.

"We live in the Royal Hotel in Lime Street," Mabel said to her. "It's not far. I'll go now and get my Father." The lady agreed.

Mabel ran back into Lime Street. Within minutes and again being careful crossing the road, she ran back through the main door of the Royal.

The man known as Peter, the Policeman, Tommy and Bill

were still struggling to get Fred out. Peter quickly explained that next to the missing railing, one other iron railing was slightly loose. The two men were pulling away at it. Peter was in his front garden pulling from that side while the Policeman pulled from the street side. All the two brothers could do was watch.

"They will get you out Fred," Tommy kept reassuring him.

Sure enough, it was getting loose but not enough to get Fred's head out.

Suddenly, they stopped.

"Listen!" the Policeman said. "Can you hear that? Sounds like horses."

They all turned around to look except for Fred of course.

A fire wagon came into view. It was being pulled by two horses. Two firemen sat in front and sitting behind them were Mabel and Father. They pulled up right in front of them. The Policeman recognised the firemen.

"Never thought I'd be glad to see you," he said.

"It's all down to this young lady," the first fireman said, pointing at Mabel.

He then introduced Father to him. Father jumped off the wagon to go and see Fred.

"I'm here son," said Father. "We'll soon have you out of there."

The two firemen jumped off, as did Mabel.

"This railing is quite loose," the Policeman explained. "We just need to pull it out so this poor lad can get free and go home."

The two firemen were quite big built men. For dangerous work like theirs, they needed to be.

"Right!" the first fireman said. "Arthur, grab that rope."

Arthur reached to the back and grabbed what looked like a towrope. His mate tied one end to the loose railing while

Arthur tied the other end to the back of the wagon. As soon as it was secure, Arthur went to the front to be with the horses.

"Ready Tom," he said.

"Okay!" his mate said. "Hang on lad. We'll soon have you out."

Father got himself, Tommy and Bill away from the railings. They stood back as did Peter and the Policeman. Mabel and Peter's wife stood back as well. All they could do now was watch.

"Now!" yelled Tom.

Arthur got the horses to start moving forward with him walking alongside. They kept going for a few yards when the rope tugged and the railing started to move.

"Keep it going!" yelled Tom.

Fred closed his eyes yet, he could feel it pulling away from him. Arthur was encouraging the horses to keep moving. More and more, the railing started to bend with the rope.

"It's coming!" Tom shouted.

A few more yards was all it needed. Arthur got the horses to start to gallop at a steady pace.

Suddenly and without warning, the railing shot out just missing Tom and clanged as it hit the back of the wagon. As soon as it did, Arthur got the horses to slow down.

"Whoa!" Arthur said to them. Eventually, they came to a stop.

The family ran back to Fred. They were overjoyed. He was finally free. He wasn't hurt, just a bit shaken up from his ordeal. Arthur came back to join them. Father was shaking hands with all of them. He couldn't thank them enough. Mabel hugged her brother.

"Are you all right?" she asked.

"Yes, I think so." Fred replied.

Suddenly, he felt something brush against his leg. He

looked down. As he did, he breathed a sigh of relief. The one cat who started all this, was looking up at him. Fred picked him up. He was just pleased to see him. After the day's events, everybody just wanted to get home. The family returned to the Royal. Father, the children and one curious cat called George.

CITY LIFE

It was a Saturday morning no different from any other. The morning routine was the same with the whole family sitting down to breakfast before getting the hotel ready for their guests and opening up. Mother would often need to buy certain things from the markets. The stall holders would set up their stalls ready to sell from as early as 8am. Mother asked Mabel and the boys to go and get some things for her from the market. So, off they went.

Mother made her way up to the parlour to get it ready. As she walked in, she looked out of the windows at the front of the hotel and managed to see the children crossing the street. She had a good view of Lime Street.

From the front windows, you look out on to a square. On all sides, there are parks, another hotel, large buildings, shops and busy markets. Here, you will see city life pass by.

Across the square stands St. George's Hall. This is a large civic building with a wide platform in front of it. The platform is a meeting place for the people to shout about anything and everything and be heard. Men will stand on wooden boxes and shout out about politics, religion and poverty. The crowd would heckle them and sometimes a fight would start. These are the poorer class people who had reasons to shout and to listen.

But Lime Street was also the place for everyone to meet and talk about the weather, their children and gossip. Summer and winter, the middle-class men always wore a bowler hat, dark suits with waistcoats and a watch and chain tucked into the waistcoat pocket. The ladies too wore fine clothes. Long skirts which went down to their high button boots, fur-collared jackets and large hats.

There were horse-drawn trams which travelled along Lime Street. They were known as Omnibuses. Horses were also still used to pull the cabs and the workmen's carts were pulled by old and tired horses who were past their working life.

It is on a Saturday that Lime Street is the place to be, especially for the children.

Standing at the junction of Lime Street and St. George's Place is the site of Professor Codman's Punch and Judy Show. Punch and Judy has delighted thousands of children here on a Saturday for over 80 years, each generation of the Codman family passing their puppeteer skills down through the family. Punch was known as Pulcino which is Italian for chick. This is why Mr Punch has a beak and a chirrupy voice which all the children love.

On the other side of Lime Street is St. John's Market. The Saturday market in Market Street is a busy and lively place. The stalls sell everything from homemade sweets to budgerigars and from clothes to fresh fish.

There are also rabbits and puppies for sale and if you wanted a chicken for dinner, you bought it while it was still alive but, if you paid the stall holder a few pennies more, he would break its neck for you.

The market is a noisy place. The noise of the birds, puppies and chickens all making themselves heard, mingled with the stall holders all shouting out to get you to buy.

The stall holders are a mixture of the middle class and the

poorer class. The women who work in the fish market are the poorer class. They will sit on upturned boxes alongside the fish baskets. These women are old before their time because of the life they lead. They look old and tired wrapped in their shawls and warm and ragged clothes.

The fish is carried by horse and cart from the docks early in the morning. The women pay for the fish and then they will have to sell their fish for pennies and try to feed their children. Most families have twelve or more children.

Some of the younger women will have a baby wrapped in a dirty shawl, lying in a wooden box next to the fish. While the mothers sell the fish, the other children play close by, barefooted.

As Mother continues to look out of the window, she can no longer see the children. As the markets are so busy, they have disappeared into the crowd. She is confident that Mabel and the boys are all right, simply buying from the market stalls what she has asked them to buy.

She can see nearly all the market traders. Mostly, poor people trying to sell what they can. This is like nearly all Saturdays. It is a busy time for the townspeople of Liverpool all year round, even in winter.

It is very much a part of city life.

ROOM 3

Mabel lay back on her pillow, her hands behind her head. Things had been rather quiet after the riots. The boys were bored but Mabel was happy. Cousin Maggie was coming to stay for a while. Maggie was two years older than Mabel and the two girls were very good friends.

There was a tap on the door. Kate came into the bedroom carrying a jug of hot water.

"Are you awake dear?" she asked. "Here's your water."

She put it down on the bedside table.

"Mustn't be late today," Kate went on. "Some more people coming." Kate left the room humming. She was a plump and happy person and the children were very fond of her.

Mabel got washed and dressed, then hurried down to the kitchen where Mother was preparing breakfast. Father had gone to fetch Maggie. Alice the kitchen maid was washing the floor when Mabel looked in to see if she could help Mother.

"Is there anything I can do?" Mabel asked, dodging Alice's mop.

Alice scowled as usual. She was never very happy at the best of times.

"Yes dear," Mother smiled. "You could take some clean sheets from the cupboard to Kate. She will be in Room 3."

Mabel took the sheets and went upstairs to the bedroom which was at the back of the hotel on the second floor.

The children didn't like Room 3, they thought it was very sinister. The boys said that something evil lived in one of the cupboards. It was rubbish of course, Mabel told herself. They just wanted to frighten her.

The room though, was dark and dreary. This was because the window was looking down onto an alleyway by the side of the hotel. The wall on the other side of the alleyway blocked the window and so, the light could not come into the room. The walls of the room were brown and when the oil lamp was lit, it would throw distorted shadows.

Of course, it was morning now and Kate was in there. She was making up two beds.

"Hello luv," said Kate. "Come to help have you? My, there will be a bit of fun downstairs tonight."

"What do you mean?" asked Mabel, putting the sheets on the bed.

"Well," Kate laughed. "You know Bill Fletcher? He is staying in this room. He is getting married on Monday. So, he will be having a few drinks tonight and with it being Saturday night, I don't doubt that there will be plenty of people to help him celebrate."

"Oh! Really?" said Mabel, jumping about in delight. Mabel liked Bill. He was a seaman and he often stayed with them. He would walk around singing. Everyone liked him.

Kate was about to give Mabel a job to do, when there was a call from the hall.

"Oh! It's Maggie," yelled Mabel. "Oh! Please, Kate."

"Be off with you," Kate said, laughing. "I can manage."

Mabel rushed downstairs and the two girls greeted each other with delight.

After lunch, the bars were closed. Mother and Father were having a rest in the sitting room. Suddenly, there was a loud knocking on the front door.

"This will be Mr Fletcher and friend no doubt," said Mother. "Well, their room is ready so they can go up."

"I'd better let them in before they knock the door down," Father groaned. "Sounds as if they have been drinking already."

Feeling a little worried, Father went downstairs and opened the door. The two seamen were in great spirits.

"Hello Harry," Bill greeted Father. "How about a little drink?"

They both stumbled into the hall. Father caught Bill as he nearly fell.

"I think you have had enough," Father said to him. "You had better go and sleep it off."

"Good idea," said Bill, cheerfully. "Come on Mac. Let's get some sleep."

The two men made their way upstairs, rather gingerly. They made a strange pair. Bill was a tall, powerfully built man with a happy-looking face. As for Mac, everyone called him just Mac. Nobody knew his first name. He was a small, thin and hunched man with massive eyebrows over deep-set eyes. However, one thing they had in common was they both knew how to drink.

Father followed them to their room and then went back to the sitting room.

"They are merry already," said Father. "God knows what they will be like by the end of the evening."

"I suppose I will never really understand why people want to get drunk when they are happy," sighed Mother. She shook her head and continued with her sewing.

The evening passed like most other Saturday evenings. Except of course, Bill and Mac were still celebrating Bill's coming wedding. The two seamen were by this time well the worse for drink.

The hotel was now closed. Father and the barman had finished clearing the bars. They made their way once more to their beds.

TRAGEDY

In Room 3 the next morning, it was Bill's friend Mac who woke up first after sleeping off all that drink from the night before. He tried to wake up Bill. But, Bill wasn't responding.

"Bill, come on mate," Mac said, shaking Bill. "Wake up."

Bill, still lying on the bed, was not moving.

It was after a second attempt, Mac realised that something was wrong. Very wrong. He dashed down to the kitchen. He could hear voices. It was Father and Mother getting breakfast ready for the guests. Mac burst in, nearly making them both jump.

"Harry!" Mac said, panicking. "Come quick. It's Bill. I can't wake up Bill. I don't think he's breathing."

"Right!" said Father. "I'll call the Doctor. Hopefully, he'll get here as soon as he can."

Later that same morning, Mabel woke with a start. She thought she heard voices. She sat up carefully, so as not to disturb Maggie who was sharing the double bed. There were voices. She slipped out of bed, put on her dressing gown and opened the door.

The noise was coming from the landing upstairs. She made her way up the stairs to find her Mother standing in the passage, looking very upset. The door to Room 3 was open and a low murmuring could be heard from inside. Mabel walked towards her mother.

"What is it?" she asked. "Is something wrong?"

Mother held up her hand to stop Mabel from coming any closer.

"Oh dear!" she said. "There has been an accident. Be a good girl and go back to your room."

At that moment, Dr White, who was the family doctor, came out of the room and looked gravely at Mother. He didn't see Mabel as she was standing in the dark end of the corridor behind him. The Doctor put his hand on Mother's arm.

"We will have to send for the police, Mrs Winslade," he murmured. "I'm afraid he is dead."

Mother put her hand over her mouth.

"Dear God," she said, very shaken. "What happened?"

"It looks as if he took some sort of powder," the Doctor explained. "A drug which he may have picked up on his travels and with the amount of drink he'd had, it killed him. There will have to be an inquest of course."

As he spoke, the Doctor turned round and saw Mabel.

"Mother, who's dead?" Mabel asked.

Suddenly very frightened, Mabel moved quickly to her mother's side. Dr White looked at Mother and smiled in reassurance. Then, he went back into the room. Mother put her arm around her daughter and hugged her.

"Oh, child," she said, hesitating. "It's Mr Fletcher. Now, please go and get the boys and get dressed. Alice will give you your breakfast and please stay in the sitting room until the police have been."

The Police soon arrived at the hotel. After speaking with the Doctor, they had to ask Mac some questions. Mac was by now really upset. They would have to calm him down first.

The children were sitting around the table except Bill who was trying to see through the keyhole in the door.

"Why can't we go out?" snorted Fred. "I'm fed up. Want to go out."

He did snort a lot did Fred.

"Well you can't," said Mabel, putting her arm around her brother. "Mother told us to stay here."

"What do you think is happening?" asked Maggie.

"I don't know," Mabel sighed. "Maybe Father will come and tell us."

Tommy was looking through the window.

"There is something happening," he said. "The Police are leaving."

The door opened and Father came in. The children waited for him to speak. He looked at them sadly.

"Now you all know what has happened," he said. "So, I don't want you to be frightened. Room 3 is now locked until Monday."

"What did the Police say, Father?" asked Mabel.

Father took Mabel and Maggie to one side of the room.

"Mr Fletcher's death was an accident but there will be an inquest," he whispered. "This means that the Police will ask a lot of questions but not to you children. Do you understand?"

The two girls nodded.

"Now, I want you both to keep the boys occupied so they will not worry," said Father.

He smiled at them and left.

"I told you," said Bill. Bill gave a long mournful moan and started pulling the most grotesque face he could possibly manage.

"Told us what?" asked Tommy.

Suddenly, Tommy was caught off guard as Bill jumped on his back. They fell on to the carpet.

"Twas the Devil," Bill gasped. "He came out of the cupboard and struck old Fletcher down dead." Bill gasped and choked from beneath Tommy as they rolled round the floor.

"The devil! The devil!" shouted a wide-eyed Fred, running around his two brothers.

"Be quiet," said Mabel. "You will have Mother here."

She was getting upset because she was in charge. The boys were reluctant but they behaved.

"Now then," Mabel continued. "It's a nice day. Let's go and ask Mother if we can go down to the Pier Head and watch the ferries coming in."

"That's boring if we can't go on one," said Bill. He protested as he sat down again at the table, kicking the leg.

"Well, let's go and see Mother anyway," said Tommy.

It seemed a good idea for them to get out for a while.

It was bad enough that Bill Fletcher had died in their home but leaving his body there all night with children in the hotel, seemed disgraceful. However, the Police had been firm about it. The body must stay there until tomorrow morning and they could then move it to the undertakers.

NEW BRIGHTON

The children, who were still thinking about going out, made their way down the passage to the kitchen. Mother was going about her jobs in a daze when they all crept in. She looked at them and wondered what on earth she could do with them.

"Mother," asked Mabel. "Could we go down to the Pier Head?"

"And go on the ferry please?" Fred asked, impatiently.

"What a good idea," said Mother, smiling at them. "Would you like sandwiches?"

"Oh! Please!" shouted the boys. Mabel nodded.

"We will be careful," said Mabel. "I promise."

In great excitement, they all got ready. They set off for the pier to take the ferry over to New Brighton. Of course, Maggie went with them.

The ferries ran across the River Mersey to and from the beach at New Brighton every hour. The children had contract tickets during the summer which Father bought them every month and they could travel as many times as they liked.

They spent a few enjoyable hours in New Brighton, during which they lost Fred in the fairground and then found him again all covered in dirt, Bill ran into the sea and got his boots wet and Maggie lost her new hair ribbons. But for all that, they had a good time.

Supper had been late that evening. The boys were tired and had gone to bed early. The two girls were washed and in their nighties. They sat on Mabel's bed and talked about the day's events. Mabel sat with legs crossed on the bed to look in the mirror and brush her hair. Suddenly, she stopped. Her hair brush in mid-air.

"Oh! That poor girl!" she gasped.

"What are you talking about?" asked Maggie.

Maggie looked at Mabel in amazement.

"The girl that Mr Fletcher was going to marry on Monday," replied Mabel, sadly. "How she must feel."

Maggie nodded in agreement. With the upset of the day, they had completely forgotten about her. The two girls sat quietly for a moment, thinking. Then, the door opened and Mother came in. She smiled at them.

"I think it is time you were settling down to sleep, don't you?" she said.

The girls got into bed. Mother tucked them in, kissed them both goodnight and left the room.

"I don't think I can go to sleep," said Maggie, nervously. "Can we leave the lamp on?"

"I think Mother will come back and turn it down when we are asleep," said Mabel, nodding.

Maggie agreed.

They both lay still in the large double bed. Their eyes closed tight. They were trying not to think about the body in Room 3 upstairs but it had been an exhausting day and very soon, they were sound asleep.

Even though the children had a good day out in New Brighton, they returned home to a sad atmosphere in the hotel. Bill Fletcher was a very well-liked man who would now be sadly missed.

THE FARMHOUSE

It was August. As always at this time of year, Mother would take the children away to Wales for a few days. Mother knew a Welsh lady but only knew her as Mrs Evans. She lived on a farm not too far from the village.

A Welsh couple, who were old friends of Mother and Father, lived in a country cottage. For one week in August, they would go away and have a holiday of their own, allowing Mother and the children to spend a few days in the cottage.

Mother needed eggs for her cooking back at the hotel and she knew that Mrs Evans could supply them. So she asked Mabel and her brothers if they would go to the farm and collect them for her while she stayed behind and cleaned up. The children were happy to do that. They set off making their way to the farm.

The farm lay back from the road. You could just see the roof over the tall hedge that grew each side of the gate.

The children had walked up the hill from the village. They walked along the driveway and into the yard.

The farm dog lay in the sun. He raised his head, watched the children, decided they were friendly and went back to sleep.

Mabel rang the funny old bell that hung over the door of the shed which acted as the shop. Nobody was there.

“Let’s explore,” said Tommy. “See if there is anyone about.”

“Good idea. Come on,” said Bill, who started off towards the house.

“Oh! Come back,” protested Mabel. “You can’t just wander around. It’s private.”

She rang the bell again.

“There must be someone about,” she said to herself.

Fred wandered into the stables but appeared again with a disgusted look on his face.

“Only a funny old carthorse in there,” he said.

Fred then stopped to take an interest in the hens who had come over to peck at his bootlaces. Mabel sighed and was wondering what to do when Bill came running back.

“Hey! The door of the house is open,” he gasped, trying to get his breath back. “We knocked but nobody come.”

“Nobody came,” corrected Mabel. “I’ll go and have a look. Fred, leave those hens alone.”

She left the basket at the shop door, then walked rather cautiously up to the farmhouse. There was smoke coming from the chimney so someone was home. Bill and Fred followed her but Tommy was nowhere to be seen. Mabel approached the door and pushed it open a little more.

“Hello!” she called. “Mrs Evans?”

At that moment, Tommy appeared from around the side of the house.

“Nobody there sis,” he said. “Maybe they are upstairs.”

“If we all shout, someone will hear, won’t they?” asked Mabel.

Tommy nodded in agreement.

“HELLO!” all the children yelled.

No answer.

“Come on,” Bill groaned. “Let’s go home. It’s nearly dinner time.” He was always thinking about his stomach.

Mabel tutted and turned her back to ignore him.

"Why leave the door open?" she asked Tommy. "I mean, anybody could steal things, couldn't they?"

"I don't think it matters about doors in the country," replied Tommy. "They all seem to do it."

"Yes," Mabel agreed. "But, still, we will just try once more because Mother did want to take some farm eggs home. Right?"

The boys nodded. Mabel gave a loud knock on the partly open door and pushed it wide open. Stepping inside, she called again.

"Mrs Evans? Are you there?"

The door had sprung back so Mabel could see right into the kitchen, and what she did see made her shriek.

The boys stood still and looked at each other. Then, Tommy shrugged his shoulders and went in after his sister. Mabel stood quite still with her hand on her mouth, horrified.

What a mess! The kitchen floor was wet with soapy water. An upturned bucket showed where the water must have come from. A huge wooden table lay on its side and sticking out from behind it was a foot. Mabel looked at Tommy.

"Shall we look?" she asked. She wasn't very keen. Tommy nodded, then hesitated, but he was the eldest boy and a boy scout and this seemed to be an emergency. He crept around the table. Then, taking a quick look, he gasped.

"It's Mrs Evans and she's hurt," he said.

Mabel, treading carefully so she didn't slip, joined her brother. Mrs Evans was lying with her head against the table. Her eyes were closed and her face was very pale. On her forehead, was a deep cut. The blood had trickled down on to the collar of her dress.

"Shall we go for help?" asked Mabel in a whisper.

Tommy nodded.

"Send Bill," he said. "He can run fast."

"What for?" said a voice from behind. Bill had crept into

the kitchen and tip-toed around the table, eyes open wide.

"Has she been murdered?" he asked, glancing nervously at Mrs Evans.

"Oh no!" Mabel replied, giving an exclamation of annoyance. "Silly. She has just had an accident. Run and fetch Mother and the Doctor if you can find him. Go quickly now."

Bill didn't have to be told twice. He was only too pleased to leave the farm and he was off like a shot.

"Wait for me!" yelled Fred. He had stayed in the doorway, too scared to go any further. Now, he ran after Bill as fast as his fat legs would let him.

"Do you think we can move her?" asked Tommy.

He walked up and down, trying to think and act like a grown up.

"We could try and get her onto a chair," suggested Mabel.

"Right!" Tommy agreed. "Now together."

The two children gently took Mrs Evans under the arms and heaved but she was rather a plump lady. All they could do was pull her into a sitting position.

"We'll never lift her," panted Tommy. "She's too heavy."

"Can we get her against a chair?" Mabel asked, sitting on a stool to get her breath back.

Tommy agreed. They heaved and pulled the lady away from the wet and, putting a cushion behind her, propped her up with her back to a chair. With that, Mrs Evans opened her eyes and groaned.

"Oh my!" she sighed, bewildered. "Where am I?"

"It's all right," said Mabel as she patted the dazed lady on the arm. "We'll help you. We are the Winslades, you know. We are staying in the village."

Mrs Evans just gave Mabel a blank look, then she sighed again. She was just happy enough that someone was there to comfort her.

"Shall I make you a cup of tea?" Mabel asked. "My brothers have gone for help. Mother will be here soon."

Without waiting for a reply which didn't come anyway, Mabel went across to a large kitchen range which had the fire and an oven. The fire was nearly out. There was a pile of logs in the large fireplace so she put one on the fire and gave it a poke with a large brass poker. Then, finding the kettle, Mabel filled it at the large stone sink which was big enough to have a bath in. She hung the kettle on the hook over the fire.

"Won't be long," she called to Mrs Evans who waved her hand in reply.

While Mabel found the cups and saucers plus the tea and milk in the old Welsh dresser, Tommy became very thoughtful.

"Do you have a medical box? I'm a Boy Scout," he said, proudly.

Mrs Evans nodded in the direction of a top cupboard. Tommy looked around and found a stool. Balanced carefully on the stool, he looked inside the cupboard. On the shelf, right in the middle of jars and bottles, was a cardboard box. He looked inside it. There was gauze, bandages and ointment. This was it.

Mabel found a small bowl and filled it up with water. Then, Tommy, very carefully so as not to hurt her, cleaned Mrs Evans's face with a piece of the gauze.

The kettle whistled and, very carefully, Mabel wrapped a tea towel around the hot handle and carried it to the dresser. She made the tea in a large brown teapot and poured a cup for Mrs Evans.

"Oh, you are a good boy," the old lady said to Tommy.

"And you too, dear," she said to Mabel. "Very good children."

She smiled at Mabel as she took the tea from her.

Tommy, now very pleased with himself, took command of the situation.

"Shall we try and clean up, do you think?" he whispered to Mabel.

She nodded. The two children helped Mrs Evans to her feet and into her big armchair.

"That's better," sighed Mrs Evans. "Glad to be off that floor. That I am."

Mabel found a mop and with Tommy's help, they managed to soak up the water. Mind you, they got their stockings and boots rather wet. With a struggle, they managed to lift the table upright.

They had just finished, when the sound of a pony and trap coming into the yard announced the arrival of Mother and the Doctor. In came Dr Jones with Mother close behind him. The Doctor was a big cheerful man with a red face and lots of whiskers.

"Now then, Blodwyn Evans," the Doctor roared. "What have you been doing then my girl?"

"Oh! Jack," Mrs Evans replied. "I did something so daft. That I did. I filled my bucket up too full, the water slopped on the floor. I slipped and then I fell. Hit my head on the table I did. Next thing I knew, was that these lovely children were here to help me. Oh! Tis lovely they are."

The children were beginning to feel just a little bit embarrassed.

Mother was so relieved to see them safe and well. Bill had arrived at the cottage, screaming his head off about the floor being covered in blood. They had finally calmed him down and managed to get some sense out of him.

The Doctor examined Mrs Evans's head.

"Well now," he said. "Whoever cleaned this up, did a good job."

He raised his eyebrows at the children.

"It was me, Sir," said Tommy, blushing with pride.

Mother smiled at Tommy. She knew how much it meant to him. As there wasn't anything else they could do, Mother and the children said goodbye and made their way back.

They were halfway back to the village when Mabel stopped suddenly and cried out.

"Oh! After all that, we forgot," she said.

Mother and Tommy looked at her.

"We forgot the eggs," she said, dramatically.

Mother started to smile. Then the smile turned into a chuckle and then into laughter.

"Oh, never mind dear," said Mother. "Let's hurry."

Still laughing, Mother cradled the two children in her arms and they walked on down the hill.

The sun was warm on their backs and the sky was so blue. Everywhere, so peaceful.

FLOSSIE

Flossie was the only daughter of George Harris who was a baker. His bakery was next door to the hardware shop owned by Uncle Bill. Flossie spent half of her time at home and half at Aunt Lizzie's place. Both Uncle Bill and Aunt Lizzie were very fond of the little girl.

Flossie was 8 years old and already a little lady. She was small for her age with red, curly hair and a cute little face. She loved it when the children were staying with Aunt Lizzie, especially Bill. He was just one year older and so they were constant companions.

One afternoon, Mabel and Tommy wanted to help Uncle Bill in the hardware shop. Fred had developed a cold so Mother made him stay indoors.

Flossie decided that she would like to pick the wild flowers that grew on the hill close by, so she and Bill set off down the road. It was a lovely day and the sun was warm on their faces. Flossie carried a basket for the flowers. They carefully crossed on the stepping stones over the shallow stream that flowed, winding around the road and past some cottages.

A little way along, they climbed over a style and made their way up the narrow path on the hill. At the top of the hill stood some huge rocks. Really, they looked more like a cave entrance. This made Bill think about the book he had received last Christmas called *St. George and the Dragon.* The cave the dragon lived in looked something like the rocks he could remember from a picture in the book.

Flossie ran on ahead while Bill sat on a large flat stone. Picking up a stick, he then proceeded to break it up into small pieces and imagined he was St. George. He would fight the dragon to save Flossie. He would do anything for Flossie. Well, almost anything. He would sooner fight the dragon than pick silly flowers.

He was still daydreaming when the little girl's voice broke into his thoughts.

"Oh look!" Flossie called, delightedly. "There's lots and lots. Aren't you going to help?" Putting the basket down, she ran to gather the flowers.

Bill gave a shrug and rather reluctantly looked around. There was a bush that looked pretty. He wandered over to have a closer look.

"Yes!" he thought. "They would do."

Being a town boy, he didn't know much about flowers. Bill grabbed a handful. Suddenly, he felt a stab of pain in his hand. He yelled and quickly dropped them again. The flowers had been growing on a prickly bush. The yell made Flossie run back.

"Oh! Let me look," she said. She took his hand. It was bleeding. Bill blinked back the tears.

"Mustn't cry," he kept thinking. Well, he was nine now and growing up quickly.

Flossie took her hankie from the pocket of her pinafore and wiped the blood away.

"Shall we go back to the stream and wash it clean?" she suggested. "That's what my Mum would do."

Her Welsh voice was very sympathetic.

Bill shook his head.

"I'll just keep the hankie on it till it stops bleeding," he said.

The two children sat on the grass and while Flossie was engrossed in playing nurse, Bill thought about the two things he wanted to do when he grew up. One was to sail around the world and the other he thought, was to be with Flossie.

"Will you love me when we grow up?" he asked suddenly, without really thinking. He then felt a bit silly. Flossie looked at him with wide eyes and then she giggled.

"I don't know," she said.

"Oh! Please say yes, will you?" Bill cried excitedly. "Go on, say yes."

Flossie didn't answer straight away. She sat with her head bent and fumbled with the hem of her dress. Then, she looked up at him shyly.

"Yes! All right, I will." She whispered.

Bill took her hand.

"Well," he said. "Now you have to say."

He stopped to think.

"You must say." He hesitated again.

"Say, I will love you when we grow up for always."

"Do I have to?" Flossie asked, wrinkling her nose.

"Yes! You must," Bill replied impatiently. "It's what grown-ups say."

"Oh! Well," Flossie sighed. "All right, I will love you."

She stopped.

"For always?" Bill asked.

"For always." Copied Flossie in a serious voice.

Then, she dropped his hand and giggled again.

"Sounds daft," she said, her Welsh accent croaking with laughter.

"On you," snorted Bill, jumping to his feet.

He looked at his hand. It had stopped bleeding but it did look dirty.

“Here’s your hankie but it’s dirty,” said Bill, handing it back. “Shall I ask Mother to wash it?”

“No, Mam will do it.” Flossie replied, putting the hankie in her pocket.

Flossie picked up her basket and then she looked at Bill.

“Do you think I should have a ring?” she asked. “You know, because I have promised.”

Bill sat down again for a moment to think. Then spotting some daisies, he picked four. While Flossie watched in surprise, Bill wove the daisies together to make a ring. He gave it to her. Flossie smiled happily and put the daisy ring in her pocket with the hankie.

“Coo-e!” came a cry.

The children looked down towards the stream. Aunt Lizzie was standing on the step of the style, waving.

“Tea!” she called.

“Come on,” said Bill. “It’s Welsh cakes for tea. I love them.” Bill took Flossie’s basket from her.

“Let’s hurry,” he said.

“I am going to learn how to make cakes,” said Flossie. “Then, I can make them for you.”

She made it sound very important.

“Great! Come on,” replied Bill. He was too hungry. The flowers all forgotten, they skipped and laughed happily down the hill.

LUCY

Mabel was happy with things but at the same time, she was a little worried. She had a friend at school called Lucy. They were not close friends, yet Mabel felt sorry for her. None of the other children would be friends with Lucy because she was what they called 'posh'. Lucy's father was a doctor and they lived in a large house in Rodney Street. This was where all the doctors lived. She didn't have any brothers or sisters and was a very lonely girl.

Lucy had asked Mabel to come around for tea and she was very pleased when Mabel said she would like to. So on Saturday afternoon, Mabel set off for Lucy's. She wore her best green velvet dress and her black button boots. She also had a green bow in her red hair. As it was getting cold now because it was at the end of October, Mabel also wore her warm, brown woollen coat.

Lucy was watching out for Mabel at an upstairs window. When she saw her coming, Lucy wanted to run down the stairs and open the front door herself, but her Mother always told her to let the maid answer the door. Lucy's mother liked to make an impression. She was such a snob.

Lucy saw Mabel coming closer to the house. She rushed straight down the stairs and opened the door before Mabel had time to ring the bell. Mabel jumped as the front door suddenly opened, then she smiled as she saw her friend. Lucy gave Mabel a hug, she was so pleased to see her. Mabel took off her coat and hung it on the large coat stand. Then she took a quick look around the large hallway. There were three doors all marked. One door was marked with the word surgery, the second was the waiting room and the third door had the word 'office' on it. Lucy took Mabel's arm.

"Let's go upstairs."

The two girls walked up a wide staircase. The stairs were carpeted in green and there were pictures on the walls. It was not like the dark, winding staircase at the Royal.

At the top of the staircase was a large sitting room. Mabel gasped when she saw it. There were two large sofas and their arm chairs were all covered in dark green velvet. There were foot stools and small tables. The walls were cream and the large windows looked out on to Rodney Street.

Just as Mabel was about to sit down, the door opened and Lucy's mother came in. She was a small yet very pretty lady with fair hair pulled back into a chignon. She wore a blue dress which hung right down to her feet. Also on the dress were cream ruffles on the long sleeves and the high neck. She smiled at Mabel.

"Hello my dear."

Mabel smiled back and gave a little curtsy. She didn't know why she did that. It was just that Mrs Sutton was the kind of lady, that any other girl or woman did a curtsy to. She had that kind of look about her. The two girls sat down on the sofa. Mrs Sutton walked across to the fireplace and pressed a bell.

A few minutes later, the maid knocked on the door and came in. She was puffing and panting. The poor girl had just ran up two flights of stairs. Her face was red and her cap was crooked.

"We will have tea in 15 minutes, Sally," said Mrs Sutton, frowning a little.

"Yes Ma'am," replied Sally, who gave a little curtsy as she left.

Mabel was fascinated by this. It was like watching a stage play. Lucy squeezed her friend's hand with embarrassment. Mabel squeezed back as if to say don't worry. Mabel was concerned about the maid bringing the tea up two flights of stairs. Lucy guessed what her friend was thinking and whispered that there was a small kitchen at the end of the hall.

Mrs Sutton sat in the chair opposite the two girls.

"Now dear," she said, smiling at Mabel. "Tell me about yourself. You live in a hotel, so my daughter tells me."

Mabel had been told by Lucy that her mother would ask her questions.

"Yes." Mabel replied. "But we do not take many guests. Just people who come in to the city on business and, of course, for the horse races at Aintree."

Lucy was trying very hard not to smile. She knew Mabel could match her mother very well.

At that moment, there was a knock on the door and the maid came in pushing a large trolley. She pushed it into the middle of the room and curtsied again and left. There were small sandwiches and a large cake on a silver dish. There was also a silver teapot and china cups and saucers. Mrs Sutton poured the tea and Lucy went to help. Mrs Sutton smiled at Mabel.

"Help yourself dear," she said, sitting down again with her cup of tea.

Mabel took a white linen napkin and a china plate and two sandwiches. As she sat down, she thought about her other friend Daisy. Daisy who wore clothes from the Rag and Bone man and had never seen a china cup and saucer in her life. Lucy put a small table between them and carried over two cups of tea.

Mrs Sutton was impressed with Mabel. Lucy could tell and was pleased. She wanted to have a friend very much and she knew her mother would have to approve. Mabel took a small bite of her sandwich and then decided it was time to ask. Lucy held her breath and waited.

"Mrs Sutton," Mabel put on her best smile. "Would it be all right for Lucy to come to my home next Saturday? It is Halloween and we are having a party. We've got duck apples and sticky buns. It will be lots of fun."

Mabel took a deep breath.

"And Lucy could stay the night if you will let her."

Lucy waited for her mother's reply. Mrs Sutton put down her cup.

"That would be lovely. Thank you, Mabel. Lucy does get lonely in this big house. I will write a note to your mother to thank her."

With that, Mrs Sutton stood up.

"Now I have an appointment," she said. "So excuse me girls and please help yourselves to the cake."

Then, with a smile, she left the room.

Lucy's mother was a very busy lady. She spent a lot of time on different charities. Mainly with those dealing with helping the poor. The two girls looked at each other and then jumping up, they did a little dance of joy. Then, with a giggle, they started on the cake.

HALLOWEEN

Mabel woke up early the next Saturday. It was Halloween and there was a lot to do. She dressed and hurried down to the kitchen. Mother was baking already. There was that wonderful smell of buns.

"Can I help?" Mabel asked.

She loved helping Mother. She wondered if Lucy helped in the kitchen but she did not think so. Mrs Sutton would not allow it. Mother's face was glowing from the range. She loved everything that involved her children.

"Of course, dear!" said Mother. "Wash your hands and find a pinafore."

Mabel made little balls of dough and put them on the large tray greased with dripping. Then, Mother put the tray in the large oven and when they were cooked, she sprinkled sugar on them.

Lucy was so excited. This was the first time that she had been to a Halloween party and she was allowed to stay the night. Herbert the butler walked her to the Royal. He rang the doorbell and Robert answered the door.

"Miss Lucy to see Miss Mabel," Herbert said as he handed Lucy's bag over to Robert. Then he walked away with his back straight and looking very serious. Lucy felt rather embarrassed but Robert just smiled.

At that moment, there was a yell and Bill and Fred came rushing down the stairs. Their faces were painted and they wore black cloaks. Behind them, Mabel was walking a little slower. She was wearing a long black skirt, white blouse and a black cape. She gave Lucy a hug.

"Come on upstairs and we will get you ready," Mabel said, laughing. "When Kate has finished with you, you will look wonderful."

Kate did her work on Lucy. They would not let her look until it was finished. Kate used chalks to do all their faces. Mabel clapped her hands with glee when it was finished.

"Lucy, you look wonderful," said Mabel. "Take a look."

She took her friend over to look at herself in the mirror. Lucy gasped. She was painted as a cat with a white face, black whiskers and black eyes, and she had a pair of black ears pinned to her hair. Kate had made them out of an old pair of mitts. To finish off, she had a black cape. Kate had been busy for weeks making the capes from an old dress of Mother's.

The coffee room looked very spooky. There were candles lit in the corners which threw shadows on to the walls. There were festive shapes made out of sheets which were hanging from the ceiling by string. Kate had made spiders out of black wool with pipe cleaners for the legs. There was just one lamp lit. On a table in the corner, there were sandwiches and cakes. There was also a tub of water with apples floating in it, and from the ceiling, a long piece of string, on the end of which was a bun covered in treacle.

Everything was ready and Robert was in charge to make sure that there was fair play and also that none of the children knocked over a candle.

The children had started to arrive. There were cousins Maggie and Annie. Friends of Bill's had also come. There was Harry Rotherham with some friends and they all had fancy costumes on. Harry was 12 years old. He had a crush on Maggie and every time he saw her, he blushed. Lucy was now getting very excited as she was making new friends. This was wonderful! It was so lovely to be accepted by such a large family. She was so lonely in her large house. It was a beautiful home but it was empty of warmth and laughter.

When all the children had gone into the coffee room, they stood in a circle around the sticky bun. Suddenly, Bill, who was up to mischief as usual, hit the bun hard and it sprung towards the door. At that moment, the door opened and Mrs Hanley stood there as the bun hit her in the face. The children all screamed with laughter while poor Mrs Hanley was in shock. Robert, who was trying hard not to laugh, rang the bell for Kate who arrived in a hurry. She thought one of the children had been hurt. She was shocked when she saw Mrs Hanley still standing there with her mouth open. The sticky bun was stuck to her hair and the fact that the old lady was slightly drunk made it all the more funny.

Robert removed the bun and Kate took Mrs Hanley away to clean her up. Lucy laughed so much, the tears streamed down her face and her makeup got smudged but she didn't care. She was having the time of her life. Everything else went well and everyone had a great time.

Later that night, as well as Lucy, Maggie and Annie would also be staying the night. The four girls were all sleeping in Mabel's double bed. Two at the top and two at the bottom. Mother came in to say goodnight. She tucked them in and turned down the gas lamp. The girls were all tired and they soon fell asleep.

The next morning, they all had breakfast in the kitchen. Lucy smiled to herself. Her mother would be horrified that her daughter was eating in the kitchen. After breakfast, Maggie and Annie were staying for the day. Robert knocked on the door. He was ready to take Lucy home. Lucy picked up her bag and thanked Mother for having her.

"You must come again Lucy," Mother said, smiling.

"Oh yes please!" Lucy replied.

She was so thrilled. At the front door, the two girls hugged. Mabel waved goodbye as Lucy and Robert walked along Lime Street. It had all gone very well.

DAISY

It was Boxing Day. Mabel, Bill and Fred had brought some Christmas food from home for Mabel's school friend Daisy and her family.

As soon as they arrived, Mabel stood in the middle of the Court. It was dark and dreary even though it was only afternoon.

The Court, as it was called, was in Renshaw Street. The houses were built in a square. The families who lived here were mostly living in poverty and had lost all hope of anything better. Some of the Courts in the city were better than others but this one was one of the poorest ones. There was a terrible smell coming from a hut in the middle of the yard. It was the lavatory and all the large families living here shared the same one.

Mabel shuddered and hurried past. Fred, who was clinging on to her coat, stopped and pulled her back.

"I don't want to go in there. Let's go home!" he cried.

"Don't be a baby," Mabel said, giving him a hug. "Look after him, Bill."

Bill nodded and took Fred's hand.

Mabel held on tightly to her basket and, with a determined look, she walked ahead to look for number 6. Treading carefully in the dirt, she counted the houses. She found number 6 at the end of the terrace. It was dark and had dirty, torn curtains at the windows. Mabel was shivering. Not because she was cold but because of what she would find inside.

The children all jumped with fright when a group of rough-looking men came into the yard. They were drunk and singing at the top of their voices. Fred hid behind Mabel and Bill moved closer to her. When the men saw the children, they stopped singing and looked at them.

Mabel felt nervous as they did look well dressed and so out of place with the area. Mabel was in her new warm, dark green coat with fur collar, her fur hat and muff. The boys wore thick jackets, breeches, warm scarves and gloves.

But the men just laughed and went on their merry way down one of the alleyways.

"Shall we knock on number 6?" asked Bill.

Mabel nodded and, just as she was about to, the door suddenly opened and a tall, thin man stood there. He was dirty and needed a shave. He was wearing a jacket, dark trousers and a dirty cap.

"What do you want?" he growled at them. He looked menacing. Fred let out a cry. Mabel stood her ground even though she was trembling.

"We have come to see Daisy," she said.

"In there," he growled again.

Pulling at his cap, he pushed past them and staggered out into the yard. The children looked at each other.

"Want to go home," cried Fred. "Don't like it here."

Bill looked through the doorway then back at his sister.

"Do we go in?" he asked.

"We have come all this way," she replied. "And we are not taking this food back home."

Mabel hesitated and then pushed the door.

"Hello!" she called. "Can we come in please?"

There was no answer.

"Hello Daisy," she called again. "It's Mabel. Are you there?"

There were hushed voices from inside the dark hall. Then, a small white face appeared around the door. It was Daisy and when she saw Mabel, she burst into tears.

"Oh! Daisy, what is wrong?" Mabel asked as she put the basket down and put her arms around her friend.

"It's my Dad," sobbed Daisy. "He has lost his job and we will all be put in the workhouse."

"You won't today," piped up Bill. "It's Christmas." Mabel gave him a look which said '*be quiet*'.

"Can we go inside?" she whispered.

Daisy wiped her eyes on her ragged shawl.

"You won't like it," she whispered back.

"It is all right, Daisy," said Mabel. "We are here to help." She looked back at Bill.

"Do you want to wait here?" she asked him.

Bill looked at the dark houses.

"No, we're coming with you," he replied, pulling Fred in and closing the door.

Mabel picked up the basket and, taking Daisy's hand, the two girls went along the dark hallway. The two boys followed close behind, Fred holding onto Mabel's coat.

The main room was very dark and cold. There was a large wooden table, a ragged sofa and two chairs. The room was lit by a gas lamp and although it was still daylight outside, not much light came through the one dirty window.

Along the hall was the scullery with a large stone sink, a small cooker and cupboards. On the wall hung a tin bath. There were some stairs which led to an upstairs room.

Mabel went further into the big room and it was then she noticed the other children. They were sitting together on the sofa, 3 boys and a small girl. They all looked at her with wide eyes. The room was cold. There wasn't a fire in the fireplace.

"I am so sorry you had to see this," Daisy whispered to Mabel.

Mabel hugged her friend.

"It is all right," she replied. "Really, it is."

Sitting on an old rocking chair was Daisy's mother. She was holding a very young baby in her arms. She looked up as the children came in. She was only young but looked old and tired. She was wearing a shabby skirt and blouse and was wrapped in a shawl which she pulled around the baby.

Daisy spoke to her Mother.

"Mum," she said. "This is my friend from school and her brothers."

"Hello Mrs Brown," said Mabel. "I hope you don't mind but we have brought you some Christmas food."

Mabel suddenly felt ashamed.

"You see," she explained. "We had too much at home and we hoped you would like some."

She felt terrible just saying that. She put the basket on the table.

Mrs Brown looked at the basket with tired eyes. The tears then started to roll down her cheeks.

"Thank you," she said. "You are so kind."

Fred pulled at Mabel's coat. He looked around at the dark corners.

"I want to go home," he whispered. "Don't like it here."

Mabel put her finger to her mouth to tell him to be quiet. Then, taking the napkins that covered the food, she put them on the table. The four children on the sofa all kept their eyes on the basket. Mabel felt like the conjurer she had had at her birthday party, about to do a magic trick.

She took out the small chicken and ham and put them on the napkins. Next came one of Mother's cakes wrapped in muslin cloth to keep it fresh, some mince pies and an apple pie. Then, right at the bottom of the basket, she took out a small parcel wrapped in fancy paper. This, she gave to Daisy.

"These are for you," said Mabel. "Merry Christmas."

Daisy took the parcel and slowly unwrapped it and out fell a pair of mittens. They were all the colours of the rainbow with pom poms on them. She laughed with pleasure.

"I will have warm hands now," she said. "Oh! Thank you."

"Kate, our-" Mabel stopped herself just in time from saying the word *housemaid*. "Our friend makes them for people."

The fact that Kate makes them for the poor out of bits of wool, Mabel kept to herself.

Both Bill and Fred were getting restless and Mabel knew they would have to go. It would be dark soon and Mother would start to worry.

"We have to go now," Mabel said, hugging her friend.

"Thank you," said Daisy.

She started to cry.

"Please don't," Mabel said to comfort her friend. "Your father will find work."

"No he won't," Daisy said, looking at her mother. "He is a drunk and we will have to live in the poor house."

Mabel was horrified. How could people live like that? She thought.

Mabel and the boys said goodbye to Daisy and her family, wished them a Merry Christmas and left.

Later that evening after the boys had gone to bed and Father was down in the bar, Mabel sat with her Mother by the fire in the parlour. She had told Mother all about Daisy and her family.

"I wish we could help," sighed Mabel. She was sitting cosy in her warm nightie and wool dressing gown and sipping at her cocoa.

Mother smiled at her eldest child.

"There are so many families like that in the city," she said. "Fathers out of work, people hungry, babies dying. One day, things will be much better. People like that will get help but it will not be for a long time."

Mabel looked into the fire.

"Oh! I do hope so," she sighed.

Mother put her knitting in her lap and looked at Mabel.

"I have thought of one way we could help for now," Mother suggested. "Tomorrow, we will look at the clothes that you and the boys have grown out of. I was going to give them to the 'Sisters of Mercy' at the Church for the poor."

Mabel smiled. "We could give them to Daisy's family," she said.

Mother nodded. Mabel clapped her hands with delight.

"Now then young lady," said Mother. "It is time for bed. We will sort this out tomorrow and I will send Robert with you this time in case there may be some trouble." Mother remembered Bill telling her about the men who had been drinking.

Mabel kissed her mother goodnight and then made her way up the stairway to the bedroom. She knew she was lucky to have a good home and a happy family but she also knew that she could help her friend and maybe give Daisy a little happiness this Christmas.

MAY DAY
1914

There is a lot of excitement in the city today. It is 1st May - May Day.

The city has a parade on this day. All the shopkeepers hire a large cart which is pulled by the wonderful shire horses.

The carts being used normally carry coal and crates of fruit from the docks. They are scrubbed and washed until they are clean. Then, the shopkeepers decorate the carts with ribbons and streamers made out of paper and spring flowers and, of course, they will advertise their shops. The children all dress up in their costumes and sit on the carts.

Mabel and the boys were really excited. Mabel was dressed as Rule Britannia, Tommy was Lord Robert, Bill was dressed as a pirate and Fred was a cat. Kate had made his cat suit out of an old fur coat of Mother's and he had whiskers painted on his face.

The Parade started at St. George's Plateau and then made its way down the city streets to the Pier Head. The Police Band led the way and there were the Mounted Police in case of trouble.

Everyone was going to enjoy this parade, it may be the last one for a while. People were worried. There was trouble in Europe and it was possible that Britain would be involved and then, they would have to go to war with Germany.

Mabel was concerned because Tommy's friend at school was German. His name was Hans and his family had a butcher's shop in the city. Mabel had told Mother about her worries.

"It will be all right dear," Mother wanted to reassure her daughter. "He is only a child. People will not blame him."

Mother was worried really. If Britain does go to war with Germany, the German children will have to be taken out of school for their own safety. But today, they would not think of such things and enjoy the parade.

Mabel and the boys were ready to go. Robert went with them across Lime Street to the Plateau. He was carrying Mabel's shield while she picked up her long dress.

Their cart was leading the parade. It was decorated in red, white and blue ribbons and the shire horses had the same coloured feathers on their bridles. It all looked wonderful. Mabel had a seat so she could sit and wave at everybody. She felt so proud.

Tommy looked for Hans and as he saw him and waved, two bigger boys started pushing Hans and calling him names. Robert saw what was happening and went to help.

"Leave him alone," he said to the bullies. The two boys looked up at Robert who was a big man. They gave Hans a last push and then ran away shouting the words 'Little German pig!'"

"Come on son," said Robert. Robert took Hans by the hand and, walking to the cart, lifted Hans up onto it as he would be riding in their cart with them.

There were cheers from the crowd as the Liverpool Police Band came marching around the corner of St. John's Lane and took their place at the head of the Parade.

Very soon, they were all ready. The Mounted Police went ahead to clear the way. The street sellers were selling flags for the children to wave.

There was a blast from the Police whistle. The band started to play and set off in marching time. The carts all followed each other in line. It was a wonderful sight. The crowds cheered and waved their flags.

Mother watched from the parlour window as the parade set off along Lime Street. She looked down at the crowds. This threat of war would not crush the spirits of the Liverpool people. While it was still possible, they would carry on with their traditions. The parade was a welcome distraction from the horrors that they were hearing about.

The women whose men would go to war put this aside for today. Today was for the children. The women had been sewing for weeks, making costumes from old curtains and sheets and just about anything they could find.

As the parade passed the Royal, Mother saw Mabel and the boys all waving to her. As she waved back, she could not stop the tears and she thanked God that her boys were not old enough to go to fight.

THE WAR BEGINS
AUGUST 1914

Mabel made her way to the kitchen. It looked as if it was going to be a nice day. She thought she would ask Mother if they could have some sandwiches and if she could take the boys to Sefton Park and have a picnic.

Father was reading the paper and as Mabel went in, he folded the paper. Leaving it on the table, he smiled at Mother who was making tea.

"I had better go and see to the bar," said Father. Patting Mabel on the head, he went out.

It was then, that Mabel saw her Mother looked upset.

"What's wrong?" Mabel asked.

Mother poured a cup of tea and sighed as she took it to the table.

"Oh, it looks like we are about to go to war," she said, sighing again. "We are waiting for Mr Asquith, the Prime Minister, to make an announcement."

She pointed to the newspaper. The headlines said that Germany had declared war on Russia on 1st August. The headlines also said that on 2nd August, German troops had taken control of Luxembourg and Germany had declared war on France on 3rd August, which was today.

Nothing else happened that day. Mabel and the boys went to the park. Everywhere you looked, there were small groups of people all talking in hushed voices. Some of the women were crying. They had sons who were of age to be enlisted into the army.

The next day, 4th August, the newspaper headlines said that German troops had marched into and invaded Belgium and were now heading towards France. In response to the German invasion of Belgium, the Prime Minister announced to the country, that the British Empire had declared war on Germany. Although the people had been waiting for this grim news, they now knew that it had really happened. It was a depressing situation.

City life carried on as usual but everyone seemed to be in a daze, wondering how long the war would last.

All the young men, some as young as 15, were rushing to join the army.

"We will show these Germans," said these young men. "We will push them back where they belong. It will be all over in 6 months."

The older men, however, knew different. They gathered in the bar at the Royal in the evening and said this to Father.

"It is going to go on and on, Harry." They would say. They were all thinking about their sons and grandsons going off to fight. Father agreed with them. They all knew in their hearts that it was going to be a long and terrible war.

HELPING THE WAR EFFORT

The schools in Liverpool were soon involved in playing their part towards the war effort. During the year, they had made contributions which amounted to £12.

With this money, they bought wool from which the older girls made socks for wounded soldiers and the younger girls made bandages from linen which was given to the school by the parents. They were all sent to the local hospitals.

The boys also played their part by collecting medicine bottles to help equip a Red Cross motor ambulance. Two of St. Luke's School teachers volunteered for military service and left to join 'The Liverpool Scottish'.

The summer had arrived and Mabel had left school. There were no guests at the Royal for the summer so Father insisted that Mother take the children to Wales for a few weeks and he and Robert would stay behind and look after the bar.

Mother asked Lucy's mother if Lucy would like to go with them. Mrs Sutton was only too happy for Lucy to go as this would leave her free to get on with her charity work for the war effort without worrying about her daughter. Lucy was thrilled!

So, one sunny morning in August, they all left Lime Street station. The station was full of soldiers all going to fight.

As the train left for Wales, Mabel and Lucy waved to the soldiers at the windows.

The younger soldiers all waved back. For some of them, it would be a last thing they would remember from home, two pretty young girls waving and wishing them good luck.

WELSH ADVENTURE

In the summer month of August, as she did every year, Mother would take the children away for a holiday in Wales. This time was a bit different as Mabel's new friend Lucy was going with them.

It was a lovely morning on the first day there, so Mabel and Lucy thought they would go for a long walk. Mother made them a packed lunch and then they set off with Mabel carrying the basket. They left the road and walked along one of the many paths, up the hill and across the fields.

It was so hard to believe that there was a war going on. It was so quiet here. The fields were covered with corn, the hill covered with wild flowers. Everywhere was green, gold and so peaceful. Cows and sheep were grazing. There was just one farmhouse down in the dip between the hills. It was like a picture book.

The girls walked for a while and then, feeling hungry, they decided to stop and have their lunch. They sat by a stream, ate their sandwiches and talked about their families.

"You are so lucky to have family here," Lucy said, wistfully.

"Where are your family?" asked Mabel.

She realised that she didn't know much about her friend at all.

"They live in London in big houses," Lucy sighed. "They are doctors."

“Do you see them much?” Mabel asked, curiously.

“Sometimes,” Lucy replied, pulling a face. “They are so stuffy and boring.”

Putting on her best boring voice, Lucy gave an impression of her Aunt.

“How are you, Lucy?” Lucy started, mimicking her Aunt. “Do you like this and do you like that?”

Mabel laughed. Lucy was so funny. Also, Mabel knew that she had a good singing voice.

“I want to go on the stage but that is just a dream,” sighed Lucy. “Could you see my Mother’s face if I told her? She would have a heart attack.”

“Yes!” Mabel replied. Mabel could see Mrs Sutton’s face. Both girls laughed at the thought.

“Shall we walk a bit further?” Mabel asked. She stood up and brushed the crumbs off her dress.

“Oh yes,” Lucy said, jumping up. She was loving every minute of this day.

The two girls walked on, talking and laughing.

Suddenly, Mabel stopped and looked back down the hill. They had been so busy talking, she hadn’t taken much notice of where they were going.

“I think we had better go back,” she said. She was starting to get worried. She looked ahead, shielding her eyes against the sun. She could not see the road. There were no houses at all, only hedges and fields. Had they walked in a straight line or did they cross? She couldn’t remember.

“Well, if we just walk right down the hill, we will find the road,” said Lucy. She was getting a little frightened. She was not used to the country.

“Yes, I suppose so,” replied Mabel. She was still looking for something she remembered passing.

“We could just ask,” said Lucy.

“Who?” said Mabel. She was still looking down the hill.

"Look!" Lucy shouted, pulling at Mabel's arm. "Smoke."

Lucy pointed. Turning around, Mabel saw the smoke. It was just visible over the top of the hill.

"A house!" they both said together.

"That smoke wasn't there a minute ago," said Mabel, looking puzzled.

"Never mind," said Lucy. "Let's go."

Running to the top of the hill, the two girls were amazed to see a small cottage on the other side. As they got closer, they could see it looked very old and run down. In fact, it looked deserted. But, there was a fire. The gate was broken and, when they pushed it open, it creaked. The garden was overgrown with weeds and wild flowers.

"What shall we do?" Lucy asked, looking at Mabel.

Mabel hesitated.

"We really need to ask." She said.

Lucy nodded and together, they walked up the path.

Like the gate, the front door was also broken and it was slightly open. Mabel knocked and as she did so, the door swung wide open. Both girls jumped. It was dark and gloomy inside. The only light was from a dirty window. The curtains were also dirty and torn.

The two girls looked at each other.

"Shall we go in?" Lucy asked, nervously.

Mabel nodded. As they walked in, they could see a wooden table and chairs. They too were dirty and looked as if they hadn't been used for a long time. It did look as if nobody lived there but there had been smoke. Mabel thought that maybe someone walking in the hills had lit a fire.

She walked further into the room and then, startled, she jumped back just missing Lucy's foot. Standing by the fireplace, was a woman. She turned and looked at the two girls. She was young and beautiful. Her dark hair was swept up on top of her head and her face was very pale. She was dressed very old fashioned in a long grey dress which hung down to the floor. She smiled but did not speak.

Lucy pushed Mabel forward and stood behind her.

"Excuse me, but can you tell us the way to the road that will take us back to the village?" Mabel asked, almost in a whisper.

The woman was still facing them and still without speaking, she raised her right arm and pointed to the left.

"Down the hill to the left," said Mabel, suddenly feeling very cold.

The woman smiled again then turned back to the fireplace.

"Thank you," said Mabel, again in a whisper.

They turned around to leave, Mabel pushing Lucy through the door.

The two girls ran as fast as they could down the hill until they could see the road through a gap in the hedge. Mabel was still clutching the basket. Pushing through the gap, they sat on the grass by the side of the road to get their breath back.

"That was really weird," Lucy gasped. "Why didn't she speak?"

"I don't know, but I felt really cold in there," replied Mabel.

Lucy nodded in agreement.

As they sat there, they heard the clip clop sound of horse's hooves. Then, over the top of the hill, came a horse and cart. As it got closer, Mabel recognized the driver. It was Mr Jenkins who had the greengrocer's shop in the town. He must have been to market. The two girls stood up and waved.

"Whoa!" Mr Jenkins shouted, stopping the cart.

"Hello young-uns," he said. "You two are a long way from home. Want a lift?"

"Yes please." Replied Mabel.

"You will have to sit on the potatoes," said Mr Jenkins. "Sorry about that."

"That's fine, Mr Jenkins," said Mabel. "Thank you."

Mabel pushed Lucy up on to the cart, then climbed up herself.

They both sat on the bags of potatoes. Then, Mr Jenkins started off down the road.

"Mr Jenkins," Mabel started to ask. "Do you know who lives in the old cottage down on the other side of the hill?"

"Cottage down the hill?" Mr Jenkins repeated. "There is only an old ruin down there. Nobody has lived there for years. Why do you ask?"

"Oh! We just saw it." Replied Mabel, squeezing Lucy's hand.

"There is quite a story," Mr Jenkins went on. "The young woman who lived there, disappeared suddenly. Of course, if you listen to gossip, they say she was murdered and her body was buried in the garden. Mind you, nobody wanted to live there after that happened."

Mabel and Lucy looked at each other. Mr Jenkins roared with laughter.

"Old Harry Tomkins was riding his horse past there late one night," he continued. "There was a storm. Went into the cottage to shelter. He swore he saw a woman sitting by the fire. Mind you, he had been drinking. Rode that poor horse so fast down the hill. Poor thing nearly dropped dead at the bottom."

Mr Jenkins, still laughing, finished the story.

"Harry hasn't touched a drop of whiskey since." He said.

As the village came into sight, Mabel whispered to Lucy.

"I don't think we should say anything, do you?" she whispered.

Lucy shook her head in agreement. They held hands tightly.

So, had they really seen a ghost or had the woman just been sheltering? Why had she not spoken to them? Mabel was not sure. Lucy, however, was thrilled to bits. This was the best holiday that she had ever had!

CHRISTMAS 1914

Mabel made her way down to the kitchen. Since the war had started they were not very busy at the Royal. This was a good thing because Mother was really worried about Tommy.

Since Tommy had come home from Scout Camp, he had been feeling unwell and had developed a cough. At the camp, there had been a storm overnight and they had all been sleeping in water. Even the Doctor who had come to see him was worried. Tommy was not very strong and the cold he had would not go away. The Doctor had told Mother to give Tommy the syrup he had left and to rub warm olive oil on his chest when he went to bed.

Mabel said hello to Kate and Alice who were cleaning the hall with a thing they called a vacuum cleaner. It was a large pair of bellows on wheels. It had a hose with a suction end and at the bottom was a pedal. Alice pushed up and down with her foot on the pedal and Kate cleaned the floor with the tube. The dust was being sucked up into a bag by the bellows.

Mabel went into the kitchen. Mother was making cocoa for Tommy. She was pleased to see her.

"Hello dear!" said Mother. "Would you take this drink up to Tommy for me? He is in the parlour." Although Mother smiled as she spoke, she looked very tired.

Mabel made her way upstairs going around Kate and Alice who were now cleaning the stairs.

Tommy was sitting by the window. He was propped up on the bed with cushions and had a rug over his legs. Mabel saw how pale he looked, but his face lit up with such a lovely smile when he saw his sister.

She put the cocoa down on the table next to him and gave him a hug. She was shocked by the way he looked. He was so thin and frail but his eyes were bright and his fair hair falling from his forehead.

Mabel took the tongs and put some coal on the fire. It had got very cold and it looked as if it would snow. They may have a white Christmas. Tommy had a book on his knee.

"Shall I read to you?" Mabel asked, smiling.

"No, let's just talk," Tommy replied, grinning at his sister. "I like talking to you. You make me laugh."

Mabel told him everything that had happened at school that week. They were getting ready for the school concert. Everyone had been forgetting their lines and had been laughing instead. The teacher had been so cross with them but the more she shouted, the more they laughed.

Mabel stood up and imitated the teacher, waving her arms about. Tommy laughed and then, suddenly, the laughing turned to coughing. Mabel gave him a drink of water from the jug by his side.

"I feel tired now. I think I will have a sleep," gasped Tommy, really out of breath. Mabel nodded. She fixed the pillows behind his head and covered him with the rug. She then gave him a quick kiss and went out closing the door.

She sat down on the stairs and hugged her knees and just couldn't stop the tears. Kate was just on her way up the stairs when she saw Mabel. She quickly ran up and sat down next to her. She gave her a hug.

"Is it Tommy dear?" Kate asked.

Mabel nodded. She dried her eyes on her pinafore. She was only 13 but she knew that something was very wrong with her brother.

"Will he get better Kate?" she asked.

"Of course he will," Kate replied. "Your Mama will look after him very well." Kate tried to assure her. But, both of them knew that Tommy was very frail.

AFTERNOON TEA AT THE ADELPHI

After talking about Tommy, Kate went to do her jobs and Mabel went back to the kitchen. Just as she walked in, there was a knock on the back door. She opened it. It was Lucy.

"Hello," said Lucy, grinning. "I am going shopping. Can you come with me?"

"Oh! I would love to," Mabel replied. She looked at her Mother.

"Can I Mother?" she asked.

"Yes of course you can," said Mother. Don't worry about Tommy for a while. Kate and I will look after him." Mother was happy to see Lucy. Her friend was just what Mabel needed right now.

The two girls set off walking down Lime Street. They looked a picture. Lucy was wearing a new coat which was blue wool and trimmed with fur, and she wore a fur hat. Mabel looked just as smart with her long, green woollen coat with matching hat and a fur muff. They both looked older than their 13 years.

"Let's go to the Adelphi for afternoon tea," Lucy suggested.

"Should we?" Mabel gasped. "It is very posh."

"Yes! Come on," replied Lucy. "My Mother knows the Manager. She has her charity meetings there."

Lucy grabbed Mabel's arm and pulled her up the steps to the very impressive hotel doors.

The Adelphi was one of Liverpool's best hotels. Mabel and Lucy walked through the swing doors into the foyer. The Manager was standing by the reception and he looked down at the two girls. He looked very formal in his morning suit. The girls hesitated, then Lucy approached him.

"Good afternoon Mr Henderson," Lucy said, politely. "I don't know if you remember me. I'm Lucy Sutton."

Mr Henderson frowned, but then broke into a smile.

"Of course I do, Lucy," he replied. "How can I help you and is your Mother well?"

"Yes she is, thank you," Lucy replied, putting on her best smile. "We would like to have tea please if we may."

"Of course," Mr Henderson said, clicking his fingers to the young waitress who was standing by the glass doors of the dining room.

"Show these young ladies to a table, Mary," he said.

Lucy nudged Mabel, who was trying hard not to giggle.

"Yes Sir," said the waitress.

The two girls followed the waitress into the dining room. The room was quite full and they felt as if every pair of eyes were watching them. They took off their coats and Mary hung them on the coat rack, but they left their hats on. It seems that ladies do not take their hats off for afternoon tea.

Mary led them to a table where they sat down. She then took their order for tea and scones.

Lucy saw some of her Mother's friends who smiled at her and she knew that by tomorrow, her Mother would know about her visit to the Adelphi.

After tea, they went Christmas shopping. Mabel had been saving her money for months to buy presents.

The girls went into Blacklers store. Mabel bought her

mother a pair of black French kid gloves for two shillings and sixpence. As Lucy wandered off to look at other things, she got her friend a Princess Mary gift book for one shilling and sixpence. Mabel also bought a lace-trimmed handkerchief for Kate, a book about ships for Bill and some puzzles for Fred. She got Tommy a lovely writing book so he could write all his favourite thoughts in it. She knew he would love that.

The girls then went into the Boots department store where Mabel got Father a gent's leather brush case. His old one was getting worn. This cost three shillings and sixpence.

With their money all spent, the girls said goodbye and Mabel made her way home.

Letting herself in through the back door, she found the kitchen empty. Mother was with Tommy. She went up to her bedroom and hid her presents and then went down to the parlour.

Opening the door quietly, she peeped in. Mother was asleep in her chair with a book on her knee. She had been reading to Tommy who was also fast asleep.

Mabel closed the door again. Mother was looking very tired and she needed some rest.

TOMMY

The last week at school went very quickly. The Christmas pageant went very well. Mother and Kate came with Bill and Fred while Father stayed with Tommy. Some of the fathers watching were in uniform. They cried as they watched their children. Very soon, they would be sailing for France. How many would not come home again?

At the end of the pageant, everyone sang 'God Save the King'. Many were in tears.

The day before Christmas Eve, Mabel and Bill decorated the Christmas tree watched by Tommy from his chair. They had all helped to make the decorations from coloured paper and beads. Kate had made an angel for the top of the tree from pipe cleaners and dressed it up in silver paper.

When they had finished, Bill went to look for Fred. Mabel sat with Tommy and took his hand. It was very hot and clammy. He looked pale and tired. He smiled at his sister.

"I am sorry," he said to her. "I haven't been able to get presents this year."

Suddenly, he had a fit of coughing. Mabel gave him a hug.

"All we want for Christmas is for you to get well," she said.

She said it as casually as she could, even though she wanted to cry. Tommy smiled again.

"I think I will have a sleep now," he said.

He closed his eyes. Mabel gave him a kiss and went out, quietly closing the door.

Christmas Eve was a cold and frosty day but the frost gave it a magical feeling. The children were hoping it would snow.

Mother and Kate were busy in the kitchen. Mother was making pies for Christmas Day and Kate was plucking the turkey. Kate was staying at the Royal for Christmas. She was on her own anyway. Her husband was away with his army unit at camp. They were on standby. Mabel came into the kitchen. Mother smiled at her daughter.

"Is Tommy all right for now?" she asked, sighing.

"He is sleeping," replied Mabel, trying to keep the worry out of her voice.

Mother looked so tired. She was not sleeping, spending a lot of time at night by Tommy's bedside. She put the pies in the oven.

"Will you keep an eye on them love?" she asked Mabel.

She wiped her hands on the towel. After that, she took off her apron.

"I will go and have a look at Tommy," she said. "Doctor White is coming to see him, just to check on him before the holiday."

As Mother left the kitchen, Kate came in looking hot and flustered.

"I have been giving everything an extra clean, so we don't have to do it over Christmas," she sighed. "Oh! I do need a cup of tea."

"I will make it," said Mabel. She went to put the copper kettle on the hob and gave the fire a poke.

They had closed the guest rooms over the holiday, because of Tommy. It would have been too much work for Mother.

As Mabel and Kate drank their tea, both deep in their thoughts, there was a knock on the back door which made them both jump. Kate opened the door. It was Doctor White. He smiled at Mabel.

"Hello my dear," he said. "I have come to see Tommy. Your Mother is expecting me. Shall I go up?"

"Yes please," Mabel replied. "Mother is with him. They are in the parlour."

The Doctor nodded and went on his way. Kate sat down again at the table and squeezed Mabel's hand.

"He will be fine," said Kate, smiling.

Yet in her heart, she knew it did not look good. A little while later, the Doctor came back.

"Mabel," he said. "Will you go to your Mother dear and Kate, could you please come with me? I need to use the telephone."

The Doctor and Kate went into the hall to the telephone. He turned the wheel and waited for the switchboard at the telephone exchange to come through.

"I am getting Tommy into a nursing home," the Doctor explained. "Mrs Winslade will not be able to cope. He needs round the clock care. He has rheumatic fever I'm afraid."

The Doctor, while still waiting for the exchange, went on.

"Kate, I understand you will be staying for a few days. That's good because the children will need you."

Kate nodded, unable to speak because the tears were running down her cheeks. The Doctor patted Kate's arm as he could see how upset she was. Just then, he was able to make contact with the nursing home.

A few minutes later, an ambulance arrived with a screech. It was very old as all the good ambulances had been sent to the war front. Two elderly men got out with a stretcher but Doctor White waved it away.

"No! That won't be needed," he said. "Mr Winslade will carry Tommy down."

Father came to the door carrying Tommy wrapped in a blanket. Mother and Mabel followed. Mother was carrying a bag for Tommy. She was going to the nursing home with him and Father would bring her home later.

Kate was wonderful. She cooked Christmas dinner with help from Mabel and even the boys helped. Mother insisted that the table was laid in the parlour as usual, even though they would have been happy to eat in the kitchen. The table looked lovely with the best lace-made tablecloth and silver candlesticks. Kate was having dinner with them but she insisted on waiting on them first.

They all sat down. Father lit the candles and they all said a prayer for Tommy. Mother and Father were taking turns to see Tommy at the nursing home.

The next two days passed quietly but on 28th December, they heard the news that Tommy had slipped away in his sleep.

The angels had called for him and he was now at peace.

FAREWELL TOMMY

Mabel opened her eyes and then closed them again tightly. How would she get through this day? Her beloved Tommy was gone. She blinked back the tears.

Pulling the quilt around her, she wanted to remember the happy times. She would miss Tommy so much. Even though he was younger than her, Mabel looked upon him as an older brother. He had always been there when she had needed him. Everyone needed somebody and Tommy had been Mabel's rock. Quiet, but strong.

But, she must be strong today for Mother's sake and look after both Bill and Fred.

There was a knock at the door and Kate came into the bedroom with a jug of hot water. Mabel sat up and hugged her knees. Kate's face was red and her eyes were puffy where she had been crying. Everyone had loved Tommy.

"I will wake the boys and get you some breakfast," said Kate, hurrying from the room.

Mabel jumped out of bed and hurried to wash and dress. It was cold in the bedroom. There would be a fire in the kitchen. It was a cold winter's day for Tommy's funeral.

It was a long, slow drive to the cemetery. As they arrived, it started to snow. Then, they saw a wonderful sight which Mabel would always remember. Tommy's scout group were lined along the driveway to the gate. They stood tall and proud in the falling snow. Mother had a little cry and then she took Father's arm. They both stood for a moment. Mother in her warm, long black coat and fur wrap. Her face was covered by the veil on her hat.

Father looked back at the children and then he put his arm around Mother as they started to walk. Mabel pulled her warm cape around her and taking Bill and Fred by the hand, they walked behind Father and Mother to the grave.

Thomas Henry Winslade, aged 11 years, was laid to rest on this day. It was 31st December 1914.

After the service, the family went back to the hotel. In the parlour, Father put some coal on the fire. Then, he walked to the window. Lime Street was quiet at the moment. It had stopped snowing and although it was only 4.00pm, it was getting dark. Of course, it would be noisy later. After all, it was New Year's Eve. The Royal, however, was closed out of respect for Tommy.

Father looked back at Mother who was asleep by the fire. She hadn't been getting a lot of rest over the last two weeks. He sighed and looked again out of the window, wondering what the new year would bring. The war, it seemed, would get worse. A lot of young men could die and for what? It seemed like such a waste of life.

He quietly left the room and went down to the kitchen where the children were having tea. Kate, who was washing the dishes, looked up as Father came in. Without saying a word, she dried her hands and left the room. Father poured himself a cup of tea from the large teapot and sat at the table with the children. Mabel looked at her Father. She didn't want to cry again. She was trying to be grown up and look after her brothers.

"Mother is resting," Father said, softly. "So I want you all to be good." He went on looking at the children. Bill nodded and took Fred's hand.

“Come on,” said Bill. “Let’s go and get out the games we got for Christmas.”

The two boys left the kitchen. Father took hold of Mabel’s hand.

“You are a little lady now and I am so proud of you,” he said, smiling at her.

Mabel blushed with pleasure. Aged 13, she did feel grown up. She knew that Mother would need her help and they all had to learn to live without Tommy. It would be hard for a while but they all would be all right. Each in their own way.

1915 - A NEW YEAR

It was New Year's Day but for Mabel, nothing would ever be the same again. Not for a long time anyway. Tommy was gone and even though she loved Bill and Fred, Tommy had been her friend as well as her brother. He had known how she felt about things and she could talk to him. He had been older than his years.

Mabel looked out of the window and sighed. It was still snowing but it was warm in the parlour. She sat on the footstool by the fire that Kate had made in the large fireplace. Her hands in her lap, she smoothed her dark green woollen dress and sighed again.

She would go and find Mother shortly but for now, she wanted to be alone. As she gazed into the fire, Mabel was thinking about the coming year. She would be 14 in the summer and would then leave school, but with the war happening, she wondered what the future would hold for them.

Mabel looked back at the window. It was snowing really hard now. The snowflakes were sticking to the window pane. Her eyes filled with tears as she thought about the snow on Tommy's grave and she made herself a promise that in the spring, she would plant lots of flowers to grow there.

There was a tap on the door and Kate came in with the coal bucket. Without saying a word, she put the bucket down by the hearth and pulled the other footstool next to Mabel. Sitting down, Kate gave her a hug. They sat there together both quietly crying. Then Mabel remembered Kate's husband. Sam was in the army and his regiment would be going away to fight very soon. Kate took a tissue from her apron pocket and blew her nose.

"Right!" she said. "I must go now. Your Mama has given me the rest of the day off to go home. My Sam is on leave." Mabel nodded and wiping her own tears, she gave Kate another hug.

"Give my love to Sam won't you?" she said.

Mabel liked Sam, he was a cheerful man. Now, he was going off to fight in a dreadful war. She was so glad that her brothers were not old enough to go.

Boys aged 14 and 15 were running away from home to join the army. Most of them would be sent home but some managed to join up. They all thought it would be a great adventure and it would be over soon.

Mabel went over to the window. It was still snowing. Lime Street looked so peaceful all covered in snow. She thought about France. Was it snowing there? Were the soldiers cold? She closed her eyes but the picture of the snow-covered fields and the blood of the wounded and the dying kept coming into her head. She thought to herself why? Oh why was this happening?

The winter months passed. The news was dreadful. More and more men were sent to fight. They were so willing to go.

The family all watched as the regiments marched down Lime Street to the docks and on to the boat that would take them off to war.

THE LUSITANIA

Spring came. Mabel kept her promise, so she and Kate went to the cemetery and planted flowers on Tommy's grave.

Spring passed and then the dreadful news came which shook up the people of Liverpool. The passenger liner *RMS Lusitania* had been sunk by a torpedo fired from a German U-boat off the coast of Ireland. It was 7th May 1915. The ship was on her way from New York to her home port of Liverpool. The *Lusitania* was the pride and joy of Liverpool. She was nicknamed Lucy. People took their children down to see the ship coming and going from the Mersey.

Everyone in the Royal's bar that night were talking in hushed but very angry voices. The question 'Why'? was on everyone's minds. The *Lusitania* was a passenger ship, not a war ship.

The news was coming through bit by bit. What the people heard was horrifying. The main questions were how many people had drowned and how many had survived. Of course, a lot of the ship's crew were Liverpool men. Their families waited anxiously for news.

The Royal became the information point because it had a telephone. It was a new and clumsy thing. Father would turn the wheel and then wait for the switchboard to come through. Of course, it was jammed with calls.

Father was able to find out the news. The *Lusitania* had only taken 20 minutes to sink. It was off the coast of Queenstown. The local fishermen had all taken their fishing boats out to help the survivors. The people of Queenstown took the survivors into their homes and gave them dry clothes and food.

The next day, Mabel, Bill and Fred watched from the windows of the hotel as people gathered together outside on St. George's Plateau. All the people of Liverpool were bound together by tragedy. Together, they all sang the seamen's hymn. The hymn went:-

Eternal Father, strong to save,
Whose arm hath bound the restless wave,
Who bids the mighty ocean deep,
Its own appointed limits keep,
Oh! hear us, when we cry to Thee,
For those in peril on the sea!

Very soon, the sorrow would turn to anger and on 9th May, the anger exploded. Mobs of nearly 3,000 people took their anger out on the Germans who lived in the city. Many Germans owned butcher's shops in and around the city. Angry crowds went on the rampage. They broke the windows, wrecked the shops inside and they even stole the meat.

German citizens were taken into custody at the police station for their own safety and protection and their children were taken out of school before they were attacked by the other children.

It was the innocents that would suffer in this terrible war and it was all because of one man who wanted power.

After the riots had calmed down, Father explained to Mabel why we were fighting Germany but she could not see why. The Kaiser and King George V were cousins. Yet despite being related, it was all about politics, greed and power.

THE SOMME

Mother was taking the children to Wales as it was now summer. They went there every summer and it seemed more important to go now that the war was on. Bill was looking forward to seeing Flossie. It was July now and during the first few days, terrible news was coming through from France.

In the bar at the Royal, the older men would sit and talk in hushed voices. Many of them with tears in their eyes as most of them had sons and grandsons who were fighting out there.

This part of the war was to be known as the Battle of the Somme. Its first day, 1st July 1916, would go down as the worst day in military history with nearly 20,000 men killed on that day.

The soldiers were all in the trenches waiting for the call. Most of these young men were in their twenties and younger. The Officer in charge would give the order to shout. He would shout the words: *"Over the top lads!"*

As soon as he did, the men would climb out charging into battle. They were running into the path of heavy gunfire. Also, it had been raining which made the fields very muddy and as the men struggled through it, they were just shot down where they ran. The men charging behind them had to climb over the bodies of their fallen comrades.

The day after the battle, the family had come back home from Wales. Bill seemed to be at a loose end. Mother was busy getting ready for the arrival of new guests and Mabel was helping, so Bill found himself doing his favourite walk down towards the river.

BILL

Bill walked down towards the River Mersey. He spent a lot of his school holidays there. He longed for the time when he would be 15 and he could go to sea as a cabin boy. Of course, even if the war was over by then, it would be some time before the great passenger ships would sail again from Liverpool.

There were ships sailing to Ireland and France but Bill wanted to go further than that. He wanted to see the world. He really wanted to sail to America. For him, it would be a big adventure.

Down by the docks there was a café where all the old seamen would meet for a chat and a cup of tea. Bill looked through the door to see if Old Jock was there and he was. He saw Bill and waved to him.

"Hello young-un. Are you coming in?" he asked. Jock was in his seventies. Nobody knew how old he really was and nobody would dare ask. He wore baggy trousers, a plain shirt with a greasy waistcoat and boots that were tied up with string. He smoked a pipe that smelt really foul. Tobacco was hard to get, so who knows what he was smoking.

Jock would tell Bill about his adventures at sea. The other old seamen in the café would listen and then tell some of their own stories. Bill loved all this. This was what he wanted to do and he would not be happy with anything else.

Of course one day, he would marry Flossie. She knew about his passion for the sea and she would be happy for him to still have a life at sea when they were married.

The old seamen talked about the war in very angry voices.

"Surely this damn war can't go on for much longer," said old Harry as he banged his fist down on the table.

"Oh! How I wish I had been able to fight."

Harry had lost two grandsons in the war. Even now, two years on in 1916, men were still fighting and dying in their hundreds. Liverpool now seemed to be full of just old men, women and children.

Bill said goodbye to his old friends and walked along the dock road. He came to the Cunard building. It was a large old building and it was the home of sailing. Going up to the large front door, Bill looked in through the glass panel. He jumped as the door suddenly opened and an elderly doorman looked at him.

"Hello son, can I help you?" he asked. Are you looking for someone?"

Bill hesitated. "No Sir!" he replied. "I am going to sea when I am old enough and I was just looking."

The doorman looked back over his shoulder into the reception.

"There's nobody about. Want to come in and have a look around?" he said, smiling.

"Oh please!" said Bill.

Bill's face lit up as he walked into the hallway. His heart beating like a drum. This was wonderful. The walls were covered with paintings of the ships with the Cunard line. There was a picture of Queen Victoria when she gave Samuel Cunard the title RMS in 1839. RMS stands for Royal Mail Service.

The doorman stood behind Bill.

"Wonderful ships aren't they?" he said. "Mind you, they

will build bigger and better ones in years to come but you can't beat the old ones."

Bill nodded in agreement, his eyes shining with excitement. He could not wait to sail on one of them. He thanked the doorman for letting him in to look around and left.

He made his way home slowly. Since Tommy had died and he was now the eldest son, he was worried that Mother and Father might try and stop him from going to sea, but they both knew what it would mean to him and that one day, it would make them proud.

Bill arrived home, letting himself in through the back door. Mother was in the kitchen as usual. She was preparing the lunch for guests. There were only two of them and they were leaving today. She smiled at Bill.

"Hello love!" said Mother. "Do you want something to eat?"

"Please!" Bill replied as he sat at the table. "I am really hungry."

Mother laughed. "Nothing changes. Cold chicken and mashed potato?"

"Great!" said Bill. He started to tell Mother where he had been. "I have been down to the river."

"I wondered if that was where you had been," said Mother.

She cut some chicken and took out a large pot of potatoes from the hob. She strained some of them and mashed them for him. Bill then told Mother about his visit to the Cunard Building. She smiled as she listened. He was so passionate about the sea and she knew that eventually, they would have to let him go when the time came. Mother was quite happy about it but at the same time sad. She would miss him and his happy-go-lucky ways.

There was a knock on the back door. Bill jumped up to answer it. Standing there in the doorway was his friend Harry.

Harry thought Bill was mad about wanting to go to sea and he told him so all the time but Bill would not be put off his dream.

"Have you had your dinner Harry?" Mother asked him, knowing very well what the answer would be.

"No, Mrs Winslade," Harry replied, pulling a face.

"Come in then, shut the door and sit down," said Mother, going back to the hob.

Harry quickly sat down at the table. He loved coming here to the Royal. There was always food on the go. After dinner, the two lads went out and hung around the city centre.

THE WAR ENDS
1918

Liverpool was waiting. It was 12th November 1918. The city centre was quiet even though there were crowds of people, all in groups waiting for the newspapers.

Yesterday's paper had said that Kaiser Wilhelm II of Germany had abdicated. Despite being the eldest grandson of Queen Victoria, he had supported Germany in the war against Britain. Also, news came through that the fighting had stopped in France.

News was slow coming through. The crowds in Lime Street spoke quietly to each other. Even the traffic wasn't moving. Everyone waited.

The news boys stood in groups. They were waiting for the van bringing the day's papers.

Father was standing in the doorway of the Royal watching and waiting. Mother, Mabel and Kate were all sitting in the kitchen. Mother was reading yesterday's paper but it didn't confirm the news.

Outside, more and more people were arriving. It looked as if everyone wanted to be with someone. This was to be celebrated together as a city. The crowds were talking in hushed voices. The paperboys hopped about, not being able to keep still. The papers were late.

Suddenly, the old newspaper van came around the corner from St. John's Lane. All eyes were watching. Everything seemed to happen in slow motion. The van rattled its way along and then stopped by the waiting news boys. The elderly driver got out of the cab and, turning to the crowds, he raised both arms up to the sky and shouted: *"It's all over! The war is over!"*

Then, moving to the back of the van, he opened the doors and proceeded to throw bundles of newspapers into the street.

At first, there was silence. Then, everyone suddenly came to life. They shouted, yelled and cheered. The men threw their caps into the air. The women hugged each other. They laughed and cried. The women cried for their men who would be coming home and those husbands and sons who would not. Kate's husband was already on his way home on a hospital ship. He had lost a leg but, he had survived the war.

Father went into the kitchen but they had already heard the cheers and knew. Mother and Kate hugged each other. Kate was crying. Mabel went to Father for a hug.

History was made. The war had ended at 11.00am on the 11th day of the 11th month, 1918.

THE FUTURE
1919

1919. The city was starting to slowly build itself up after the war.

Mabel and Bill had now left school and were thinking about the future. Fred still had a year to go. Bill had already decided that his future would be at sea. Mother was worried about Bill's obsession for the sea. She would think about the *Titanic* and the *Lusitania.* One sunk by nature and the other by war.

But, nothing would put Bill off his dream. He had learnt to swim in the sea at New Brighton.

"I will be all right," he told Mother. "If the ship sinks, I can swim and help to save people."

Mother thought that swimming in the sea at New Brighton was a bit different from the ocean but she kept those thoughts to herself.

A lot of seamen stayed at the Royal and Bill would often listen to their tales of adventures at sea. The places they had been to and the people who lived there. Bill would talk about it all the time to his friend Harry Rotherham but Harry wasn't really interested. He was older than Bill and only talked about girls, especially Maggie who he thought was really nice.

Of course, Bill was interested in girls but knew that Flossie was the only girl for him. She was 14 and a lovely young girl. Bill kept her photograph with him. He would take it to sea, make his fortune and then come home and ask Flossie to marry him. That was what he wanted to do.

Father was not happy about Bill's obsession for the sea either and would try and put him off at every opportunity. Father wanted Bill to take an interest in the running of the hotel.

"He should be here helping us," Father moaned to Mother.

Mother would not get into an argument about this but she was worried too.

MABEL

Mabel closed the door to the Royal behind her. The sun was shining. It was a lovely day in May, she was going to Tommy's grave and she was carrying a plant. She had kept her promise and went every year.

The year is 1919. The war had been over for nearly a year now and on 7th June, Mabel would be 18 years old.

She crossed the road and waited for the tram to take her to West Derby Cemetery. Lime Street was busy. It was a Saturday morning and people were hurrying about, shopping and meeting friends, stopping to chat and having coffee at the pavement cafés. They had all been closed during the war and it was nice to see things were slowly getting back to the way they had once been.

There was still a lot of sadness about. Families coming to terms with the loss of a loved one. But, the people of Liverpool were strong and they would come back from their sorrow even stronger.

Mabel made her way through the cemetery to the grave. She pulled the weeds from the plants she had put there last year, then, taking her small trowel from her bag, she put in the new plant. She sat for a while and told Tommy everything that had happened in the last year.

"Bill is at sea as a cabin boy now," Mabel said to Tommy.

"He is nearly 15. Mother worries about him but a friend of Father's is on the same ship and has promised to keep an eye on him."

Mabel stopped and looked around. She was talking aloud but there were not many people about.

"Fred is still at school," she went on. "He is doing very well. Oh! Kate's husband is finally home after the war. He has lost part of a leg. It was blown off and he now has a wooden stump. Father is going to give him some work at the Royal."

Mabel walked over to the pump and got some water. As she watered the plants, people passed by and nodded at her. She smiled back. She really looked lovely today. She was wearing a pale blue dress, still with the fashionable length to her ankles. Her long red hair was in a roll around her head. She had pinned a pearl comb in her hair. It was a present from Mother on her 17th birthday. Mabel sat down again and told Tommy about Lucy.

"Lucy is training to be a nurse," she said. "But she still sings at her Mother's charities and is becoming well known. I don't know what happened to Daisy." Mabel sighed and thought about it. She had tried to find out about Daisy but nobody knew what had happened to her.

Daisy's father had been killed in an accident. He had been drunk and had walked out in front of a horse and cart. Her Mother had also died of pneumonia and nobody knew what had happened to the other children. Daisy had left the home aged just 14 and disappeared. Mabel really wished nice things could have happened for Daisy. She'd had an awful life.

Mabel stood up and thought she had better get home. She sighed and patted Tommy's headstone.

"Goodbye dear brother until next time," she said.

She felt tears coming, but she brushed them away. Tommy would have grown into such a handsome man. Tall with fair hair and a lovely smile.

Enough sorrow. Picking up her bag, she walked to catch the tram back to the city.

Arriving home, Mabel walked through the main door of the Royal. She passed the bar. Father was busy so she went along to the kitchen. Mother was probably resting and Fred was out with friends. As she thought she would make a cup of tea, there was a knock on the back door. She hesitated as only friends and tradesmen came to the back door.

Opening the door, she stepped back in surprise. There was a tall, well-dressed man standing there.

"Hello," he said. "I have come to see Mr Winslade about the barman's job."

"Oh!" said Mabel, opening the door wider. "Please come in."

"Thank you," he said. He stepped into the kitchen. He was wearing a grey suit, white shirt and tie and he had a watch and chain on his waistcoat.

The stranger smiled. He had a lovely smile, Mabel thought. He was a pleasant looking man with dark hair and a lean face.

"My name is Joseph," he said, holding out his hand. "Joseph O'Donovan."

Mabel shook his hand. She felt very shy with this stranger, but at the same time she suddenly had a feeling that she was looking at her future.

EPILOGUE

The Royal went on for some years as a hotel.

After Father and Mother retired, the Royal became a public house.

The building was finally knocked down in 1967 to make way for a larger entrance to Lime Street station.

Father died in 1932 aged 66 years.

Mother died in 1964 aged 88 years.

Both were buried with Tommy.

Mabel married Joseph and had one daughter — Mabel Doreen.

Bill married Flossie. They had two sons and two daughters:- Thornley, Claude, Pauline and Anne.

Bill finally got to follow his dream and go to work at sea. He worked on the famous ocean liner, the *Queen Mary*. He sailed around the world and for many years worked as the head wine steward serving passengers, including Winston Churchill in the ship's famous Verandah Grill restaurant. Later on, his son Claude got to follow in his father's footsteps and also worked on board the same ship.

Fred married Doris. They had no children, but they did have 3 cats.

L-R: Harry, Bill, Flossie, Jane,
(the baby is Thornley, Bill and Flossie's first son)
Fred and Mabel.